CHER HAMPTON

# 7-Week Relationship Therapy Workbook for Couples

*Your Hands-On Guide to Reignite Your Spark, Build Trust, and Create a Lasting Love Story, with Essential Communication and Connection Strategies*

*Copyright © 2024 by Cher Hampton*

*All rights reserved. No part of this publication may be reproduced, stored or transmitted in any form or by any means, electronic, mechanical, photocopying, recording, scanning, or otherwise without written permission from the publisher. It is illegal to copy this book, post it to a website, or distribute it by any other means without permission.*

*Under no circumstances will any blame or legal responsibility be held against the publisher, or author, for any damages, reparation, or monetary loss due to the information contained within this book, either directly or indirectly.*

*Disclaimer Notice:*

*Please note the information contained within this document is for educational and entertainment purposes only. All effort has been executed to present accurate, up-to-date, reliable, and complete information. No warranties of any kind are declared or implied. Readers acknowledge that the author is not engaged in the rendering of legal, financial, medical, or professional advice. The content within this book has been derived from various sources. Please consult a licensed professional before attempting any techniques outlined in this book.*

*By reading this document, the reader agrees that under no circumstances is the author responsible for any losses, direct or indirect, that are incurred as a result of the use of the information contained within this document, including, but not limited to, errors, omissions, or inaccuracies.*

*First edition*

*This book was professionally typeset on Reedsy.
Find out more at reedsy.com*

# Contents

| | |
|---|---|
| *Introduction* | iv |
| Week 1: Foundations of Connection | 1 |
| Week 2: Effective Communication | 27 |
| Week 3: Understanding Your Love Language | 44 |
| Week 4: Building Trust | 67 |
| Week 5: Intimacy and Connection | 84 |
| Week 6: Overcoming Challenges | 95 |
| Week 7: Creating a Lasting Love Story | 116 |
| *Bonus: Your Free Gifts* | 131 |
| *Conclusion* | 133 |
| *References* | 135 |

# Introduction

Love. The thing that makes the world go round. The thing that makes our hearts flutter like butterflies. But love, as I have come to learn more about it, is all about curiosity. When you experience a curious kind of love, it shows interest in you by asking how you're doing and what you need. It makes an effort to be involved in your life. However, many of us tend to grow too comfortable in our relationships and stop putting in the same effort as we used to. That initial flame that burned with the intensity of our curiosity can sometimes dwindle to a steady glow, no less warm but perhaps less illuminating. This is the natural ebb and flow of a long-term relationship, but within this transition lies a pivotal question: How do we keep the flame alive?

The answer, much like love itself, is complex and multifaceted, but at its core, it is about maintaining and nurturing the curiosity that brought you together. It's about continuing to ask, "Who are you today?" because the truth is, we are all constantly evolving. The person you fell in love with years ago is not the same person you wake up to each morning. They have grown, changed, and experienced life in ways that may have altered their perspective, and so have you.

In this workbook, we will explore the avenues of communication and understanding that are essential for a thriving partnership. We will delve into the art of listening—not just hearing but truly understanding what your partner is saying. We will practice empathy, putting ourselves in our partner's shoes, feeling what they feel, and seeing the world from their vantage point.

But curiosity doesn't stop at conversation. It extends into every aspect of your shared lives. It's in the way you support each other's dreams, how you play and laugh together, and how you face challenges as a united front. It's in the small daily gestures and the grand romantic overtures. It's in the way you show up for each other, day after day, with the intention to love, learn, and grow together.

This workbook is more than just a series of exercises; it's a journey. A journey back to that place where your love first took root—where you looked into each other's eyes and saw a world of possibilities. It's a commitment to not just recall that feeling but to live it, rekindle it, and let it transform you both.

As we embark on this journey, remember that there is no one-size-fits-all approach to love and relationships. Each chapter is designed to be a stepping stone, but it is you who will walk the path. Your relationship is unique, and the way you use this workbook should be just as unique. Take your time with each section, be honest with each other, and most importantly, be open to what you may discover.

In the end, the kind of love that lasts is the kind that's not afraid to ask questions, seek answers, and embrace change. It's a love that's alive it breathes and grows with each passing day. It's a love that's curious, always seeking to understand more deeply and connect more fully. It's this kind of love that we will cultivate together through the pages of this workbook.

So let's go, hand in hand, with open hearts and minds, ready to rediscover the curiosity that makes love truly extraordinary. Your relationship is a beautiful masterpiece in progress, and together you have the power to paint a picture that grows more beautiful with each stroke of understanding, compassion, and, of course, curiosity.

# Week 1: Foundations of Connection

*"Invisible threads are the strongest ties."*

— FRIEDRICH NIETZSCHE

Connection is a thread that weaves us all together. It is as intrinsic to our well-being as air, water, and nourishment. In a society that can often seem fragmented and isolating, the bonds we share with our partners offer a sanctuary of understanding and mutual respect. This profound sense of togetherness not only fortifies us against life's challenges but also amplifies the joys and triumphs we encounter along the way. Striving for a deep connection with your partner is not just about the blissful moments or the shared laughter that echoes through the hallways of your lives. It is about cultivating a foundation so robust that it can withstand the tremors of disagreement and the weight of sorrow. It is about the silent understanding that passes between you when words fall short and the gentle touch that says, "I'm here" without uttering a syllable.

In this section, we explore the bedrock of connection. We'll closely examine communication, not just as a way of exchanging information but as a dance of intimacy that allows you to truly see and be seen by your partner. We'll uncover the power of vulnerability, the courage to bare your soul, and the strength it takes to embrace your partner's truth. Together, we'll learn how empathy can bridge the gap between separate worlds, creating a shared space where compassion reigns supreme.

The foundation of connection is also built upon shared values and goals. When you and your partner are aligned in your deepest convictions, you create a compass that guides your relationship through any storm. This alignment doesn't mean losing your individuality; on the contrary, it's about honoring each other's unique perspectives and using them to enrich the collective vision of your future.

Let's not overlook the significance of trust—the cornerstone of any relationship. Trust is earned and nurtured over time through consistent actions and unwavering support; it is the safety net that allows you to leap into the unknown, knowing that your partner will be there to catch you if you fall. In this space of trust, love blossoms, and with it, the confidence to tackle life's adventures side by side.

Lastly, we'll examine the rituals of connection—those small but mighty acts of love that become the heartbeat of your relationship. That could be a morning kiss, a nightly gratitude practice, or a weekly date night. These rituals serve as constant reminders of your commitment and the love that grows with each passing day.

## Defining Your Relationship

Our relationships become that much more intimate and healthy when we are not afraid to show our most vulnerable sides. I believe in the notion that it is better to let your guard down, let yourself be fully seen, and express everything instead of just simply bottling everything up on the inside, even when you feel like it might lead to an argument. When you are transparent, you are open, and that is vulnerability, which is the bedrock of intimacy. Things may get bumpy when you talk about those uncomfortable things, but in the long run, it leads to a stronger foundation for the relationship. The vulnerable moments are the moments that help to heal the parts within you and the other person that otherwise would not have been possible. So, on any given occasion, when you have the choice, choose real intimacy; don't be afraid to let your guard down.

Now, I want you to meet Ethan and Jessica. They met in the 21st century way and are one of those few lucky stories where swiping right led to something truly meaningful. Their connection was instantaneous, and for a while, it seemed like they were the perfect couple. They shared a love for adventure, a passion for good food, and a mutual respect for each other's ambitions. They were the envy of their friends and the embodiment of #relationshipgoals.

However, as time went by, the initial spark began to dim. Work demands and personal ambitions started to take precedence, and the once effortless connection between them began to feel strained. They found themselves caught in the relentless whirlwind of modern life, and as the days turned into weeks and then months, they realized that they were drifting apart.

It started with little things. The spontaneous weekend getaways turned into meticulously planned outings, and their conversations became more about to-do lists than shared dreams. They both felt the growing distance but were unsure of how to bridge the gap. They couldn't shake the feeling that they were losing something precious, something they had fought so hard to build.

One evening, as they sat in silence after yet another mundane day, Ethan broke the tension by suggesting they take a break from their routines and spend a weekend at a secluded cabin in the woods. Jessica hesitated at first, but deep down, she knew that something needed to change. They packed their bags and embarked on a journey that would alter the course of their relationship.

While in the tranquility of nature, they found themselves opening up in ways they hadn't in a long time. They shared their fears, their frustrations, and their unspoken desires. They laughed, they cried, and they rediscovered the reasons they fell in love in the first place. It was during those quiet moments by the crackling fireplace that they realized the importance of introspection and communication in a relationship.

As they returned to their everyday lives, they made a vow to make a conscious effort to defog their relationship. They set aside time for each other, prioritized open and honest conversations, and embraced the imperfections that made their love unique. They learned that a strong relationship requires work, patience, and a willingness to adapt to the ever-changing tides of life.

In a very big and profound way, the story serves as a reminder that even the strongest of bonds can falter if left unattended, but with introspection and a shared commitment to growth, love can prevail.

## Reflecting on the Milestones of Your Relationship

Your relationship with your partner is a work in progress because you and your partner are two works in progress. You are both people with goals, dreams, and visions that are naturally bound to change, but that does not mean that your relationship has to suffer. In fact, this ever-evolving nature of yourselves is the very thing that can help strengthen your relationship. So, in this moment, I want you and your other to prepare yourself for a little exercise that will help you find the clarification that Jessica and Ethan got.

### *Step 1: Travel back and look at the history of your relationship.*

Do this individually, and during this, you will think about the significant moments in your relationship. Think about the positive and challenging milestones that shaped you. How did those bring you to where you are today?

## *Step 2: Think thoroughly about each of your individual dreams and goals.*

You are both people outside of the relationship. Write down your current dreams and vision for your lives. When doing this, take into consideration your personal aspirations, career ambitions, and all of the things that bring you joy and fulfillment. Think about how each of your individualistic goals have evolved over time and how they could possibly continue to change.

## *Step 3: Map out the shared vision and goals.*

Sit down together and talk through those visions and goals that have been the foundation of your relationship. What are the things that you hold near and dear to your hearts? What are common aspirations? Make note of the areas where your individual goals might align and where they might diverge. This is an opportunity for both of you to be honest and open with one another. Talk about your individual goals and how they align with the vision that you have of your future. How can you both support one another as you each pursue your individual goals and ambitions? What are potential challenges that may arise, and how can you work on overcoming those as a team?

## *Step 4: Talk about what relationship goals are to you.*

These goals should consist of the practical aspects of your relationship and the emotional connection that you guys want to maintain. Think about things such as communication, quality time, and mutual support.

## *Step 5: Work on your action plan.*

How are you both to work on these goals that you have just discussed? How are you going to hold each other accountable? This plan that you are creating should serve as the roadmap to achieving the growth and the connection that you desire.

# Recognizing Negative Relationship Cycles

Here are four life-changing relationship truths that I think you need to hear.

1. You cannot persuade someone to love you, nor can you force them to change their own inherent unhealthy behaviors.

2. Doubtful thoughts, such as wanting to leave the person, will come and go when you and your partner feel disconnected, but that doesn't mean that you cannot work on that.

3. Feelings for a person or being in love with them are not enough to keep a relationship going. Maturity, safety, and consistency are all needed, matching words with action.

4. The relationship that you have with yourself is going to influence and impact how you show up for your partner.

A lot of the time, our relationships fail, not because we have fallen out of love but rather because we keep repeating unhealthy and unproductive relationship patterns that are harmful to us and our partners. These negative relationship cycles often creep up on us in various forms, but they come from a lack of effective communication, unmet emotional needs, and unresolved conflicts. Therefore, you may find yourselves trapped in repetitive behaviors that eat away trust, intimacy, and overall relationship satisfaction.

One of the most common negative relationship cycles is the "blame game." "Oh, but you always do this," or "It's not me, it's always you." In this pattern, you engage in a cycle of assigning blame, often without taking personal responsibility for your actions or contributions to the issues at hand. This can lead to defensiveness, resentment, and a breakdown in open communication. Over time, this creates an atmosphere of hostility and undermines the sense of partnership within the relationship.

Let's not forget about "the silent treatment." A lot of the time, we think that withholding communication or affection will make the other partner see where they are at fault, but in all honesty, this just creates more division because one or both of you may withdraw emotionally and refuse to engage in meaningful communication. This silent treatment isolates and makes us feel rejected, ultimately deepening the divide. Without open dialogue, issues continue to hang, and the emotional distance grows, perpetuating the cycle of silence and emotional disconnection.

Also, the "power struggle" cycle can arise when we engage in a constant battle for control and dominance within the relationship. This struggle for power can make its presence known in various ways, such as competing for decision-making authority, seeking to undermine the other's autonomy, or engaging in passive-aggressive behaviors to assert dominance. The power struggle cycle erodes trust and mutual respect, creating an environment of tension and discord.

Additionally, the "emotional distancing" cycle can emerge when vulnerability and intimacy are rarely expressed. This cycle is characterized by a gradual withdrawal from emotional connection, often due to fear of rejection or past emotional wounds. You become guarded, avoiding meaningful conversations or expressions of affection, which can lead to emotional neglect and a sense of disconnect.

These negative cycles are often fueled by specific behaviors that contribute to their perpetuation. It is things like a lack of active listening, deflection of personal responsibility, avoidance of conflict resolution, emotional volatility, and an unwillingness to acknowledge and address underlying issues. These behaviors can create a toxic dynamic that undermines the foundation of the relationship and messes with the potential for growth and mutual fulfillment.

A great deal of research talks about how the quality of our relationships can contribute to the quality of our lives, but honestly, I choose to believe that there needs to be more out there about the way we are with ourselves. This is how I have it all laid out in my mind: A healthy relationship with the self equals a healthy relationship with others (our partners), which is equal to a good quality of life. So, what do we need to do to make sure that we are safe and healthy partners for our people?

Firstly, we need to work on our own emotional and mental stability. This means that we need to have a good understanding of our own emotions, thoughts, and behaviors; we need to be aware of our own patterns and triggers and learn how to manage them in a healthy way because this is what will help us to be more self-aware and emotionally available for our partners.

Secondly, we need to work on our communication skills. Communication is key in any relationship, and it is important to be able to express ourselves honestly and effectively. We need to learn how to listen actively, show empathy, and communicate our needs and boundaries in a clear and respectful way. This will help to create a safe and open space for our partners to communicate with us as well.

Thirdly, we compassionately allow ourselves to be as human as we can. This involves treating ourselves with kindness, acceptance, and forgiveness. When we have a healthy relationship with ourselves, we are more likely to be patient, understanding, and compassionate toward our partners as well. This will help to create a more loving and supportive environment for our relationships to thrive in.

Finally, we need to be willing to do our growth work. This means being open to feedback, seeking personal growth opportunities, and taking responsibility for our own actions and behaviors. When we are committed to our own personal growth, we are more likely to be open, curious, and empathetic toward our partners as well.

Think about what you do and how you respond when a little conflict arises.

Is it productive for resolving the conflict, or is it just going to make it that much worse?

## Relationship Foundations

Imagine that you are a long-distance runner, and you have been working hard for months to build your strength and endurance. Even though you have been training hard, running itself never becomes easier. Rather, you become stronger and better equipped to handle the physical demands of running.

Similarly, relationships can be challenging and come with their own set of difficulties. However, as we gain more experience and learn from our past mistakes, we become better equipped to handle the challenges that relationships sometimes throw at us. Although relationships may not necessarily become easier, we become more skilled at navigating through them and dealing with whatever comes our way.

Relationships require more than love, romance, and strong feelings. You cannot just plant seeds anywhere and hope that beautiful flowers are going to grow from there. The garden needs to be tended to. It needs to be nourished and plucked of weeds regularly.

A relationship is a commitment to consistently show up for one another, offering your energy day by day, moment by moment. It requires careful consideration of each other's needs and the impact that your decisions will have on the other person. When both partners invest hard work and effort into the relationship, it can be incredibly rewarding. The love that you build together becomes the essence of your existence, reflecting the deep desire for true and unconditional love.

This kind of love is not shallow or self-absorbed but rather one that has seen both the light and the dark. It brings out the best in you while also exposing your deepest wounds. A loving relationship requires a lifetime of work, but it is worth it. It teaches you the meaning of generosity, selflessness, appreciation, friendship, resilience, forgiveness, and the full expansive expression of the human essence.

When you love someone, it's much more than just becoming a couple. It's an energetic union that shapes the way you experience life and perceive the world around you. It is a blessing to know someone so deeply and to share all that you are becoming with them. Although the journey may have detours, if both partners are willing, you can always trace the map back to each other's hearts. These are the foundations that can make the path ahead a little easier.

## *Empathy*

More than simply understanding how the other person is feeling, empathy is about leaving your own thoughts and feelings at the door in order to step into the world of the other person and truly feel the emotions that they are feeling and to see the world as they see it.

if you read the dictionary, it will tell you that empathy is a way of relating to another person's emotions and feelings, but for me, that is a little too surface-level. I like to say that it is a special way of getting to know each other and those around us and our partners, attuning to and understanding their needs. When it is extended, it rescues us from those crippling feelings of loneliness.

Being heard empathetically isn't just about being listened to and understood; it's about having another person care about you deeply enough to step into your world, your pain, and your memories right beside you.

## Intimacy

Choosing people who choose us with both their actions and their words is a game changer in relationships. Intimacy can look like:

- crying in their arms when everything just feels too much and is too heavy
- vision planning together and talking about the future
- knowing that you were the first one they called when they received exciting news
- sharing about the pains from your past and how you are working on healing those wounds
- accepting ownership of those instances where you were wrong, apologizing, and taking the necessary steps to ensure that it doesn't happen again
- showing the vulnerable sides of you that others may not have access to
- engaging in play together, trying new things, and going on adventures together
- making sure that each of your physical needs are met as well
- consistently showing up, even on the days when it would be easier not to

Creating this kind of intimacy requires a conscious and deliberate decision to prioritize our partner and our relationship. It requires us to be aware of our own needs and desires as well as those of our partner. When we choose to show up for our partner consistently, even on the tough days, we create a foundation of trust and love that can withstand anything life throws our way.

## Trust

In any relationship, trust is the foundation which everything else is built upon. It's the glue that holds everything together and the key to building a healthy and lasting connection. When we trust our partner, we feel safe, secure, and supported. We know that we can count on them, no matter what.

Trust says that I will show up for you when it matters most. It's about being reliable, consistent, and dependable. When we trust our partner, we know that they will be there for us, even when things get tough. We can rely on them to have our back and support us through thick and thin.

Another essential aspect of trust is confidentiality. We all have things that we want to keep private, and when we share them with our partner, we need to know that they will keep our secrets safe. Trust says that I will not use the things that you tell me in confidence against you. It's the knowledge that we can be vulnerable with our partner and that they will not judge us or use our vulnerabilities against us.

Trust is also about honesty and transparency. It's about being able to communicate openly and honestly, even when it's uncomfortable or challenging. When we trust our partner, we know that they will be truthful with us, even when the truth is hard to hear.

Building trust takes time and effort, and it requires both partners to be committed to the relationship. So remind yourself that it's built on reliability, confidentiality, honesty, and forgiveness. When we trust our partner, we feel safe, secure, and supported, and we know that our relationship is built to last.

## *Accountability*

When we hear people talk about relationships, they often use the phrase "showing up." In the context of relationships, "showing up" means being accountable, taking responsibility, and being present for our partner. It's about being there for them emotionally, physically, and mentally. Here is 'showing up' used in context in five different ways:

- **Being there with them:** Presence is an important thing in relationships. Being present means giving our full attention to our partner. It's about being in the moment and focusing on the conversation. When we are present, we are actively listening and in the moment with our partner. We are not distracted by our phones or other things happening around us.

- **Honoring commitments:** Honoring commitments means doing what we say we will do. We don't flake or breadcrumb them. It's about being reliable and following through on our promises. When we honor our commitments, we build trust with our partner. They know that they can count on us to do what we say we will do.

- **Taking responsibility:** Own your part in the relationship. It's about acknowledging our mistakes and working to make things right. When we take responsibility, we show our partner that we are committed to the relationship and willing to work through challenges.

- **Being supportive:** Being supportive means being there for our partner when they need us. We carry them in ways that they cannot carry themselves. It's about offering a listening ear, a shoulder to cry on, or a helping hand. When we are supportive, we show our partner that we care about them and are invested in their well-being. You are essentially saying, "You're worth the time. I'm here if you need me."

- **Communicating effectively:** Communicating effectively means being clear and honest with our partner. It's about expressing our thoughts and feelings in a way that our partner can understand. When we communicate effectively, we avoid misunderstandings and build intimacy with our partner.

In order to "show up" for our partner, we need to be accountable. Accountability is about taking responsibility for our actions and being willing to own up to our mistakes. It's about being honest with ourselves and our partner about our intentions and motives. When we are accountable, we create a safe and trusting environment in our relationship.

Accountability is also a boundary-setting practice. Boundaries are important in any relationship because they help us to establish what is and isn't acceptable behavior. When we set boundaries, we are communicating our needs and expectations to our partner. It's important to remember that boundaries are not meant to control our partner. Rather, they are meant to create a safe and respectful space for both partners to thrive.

In order to be accountable, we need to be willing to apologize when we fall short. Apologizing is not always easy, but it's the bedrock of accountability. When we apologize, we acknowledge the hurt that we have caused our partner and take responsibility for our actions. A genuine apology can go a long way in repairing a relationship and rebuilding trust.

One small but powerful exercise that can help you stay accountable to your partner is to set specific goals together and track your progress. Start by discussing your individual goals and then identify a few that you can work on together as a couple. Next, break down each goal into smaller, actionable steps that you can take on a daily or weekly basis. This will help you stay focused and motivated as you work toward achieving your goal. Then, set up a system for tracking your progress. You can use a shared calendar, a habit-tracking app, or create a physical chart to mark off your progress. Make sure to check in with each other regularly and discuss your progress toward your goals.

This may not seem like much, but the act of checking in regularly with one another will strengthen your bond in ways that you could never have imagined.

## Emotional Safety

Without emotional safety, chemistry, attraction, and compatibility go out the door. You need to feel safe if you want to build a life with someone. Otherwise, you will just exist in the confines of their reality and become a shell of who you are.

When we enter relationships, we are basically yearning for connection, understanding, and, of course, emotional safety. We want to feel seen, heard, and cared for by our partner. So, if we don't feel safe enough to communicate freely without judgment or dismissal, that relationship slowly erodes our self-worth and our well-being. The unresolved conflict and pent-up frustrations further damage the bond, so instead of a nurturing relationship, we find ourselves trapped in a distressing attachment or traumatic bond.

We owe it to ourselves and our partners to build relationships that are rooted in compassion, attentive and active listening without judgment, respect for each other's autonomy, and willingness for reconciliation. Every voice deserves to be heard. Everyone deserves consideration, and even disagreements deserve air time and resolution.

Connection thrives when no one dominates, silences, or diminishes the other person. Healthy relationships empower both people to heal, share their inner truths, stand firmly in their worth, and resolve issues with fairness and empathy. We nurture our bonds by offering each other a safe harbor for growth and healing.

Here are some gentle reminders of what emotional safety looks like in the context of our relationships:

- making sure that your partner knows that you are a priority to them
- having a partner who reflects on and validates your emotions and experiences, and you are able to do the same for them as well
- having firm, healthy boundaries in place
- being able to accept feedback without becoming defensive
- having time to each engage in your own interests and hobbies, and continuously encouraging each other to do the same
- having a partner who recognizes their own maladaptive behaviors and

putting effort into healing and personal growth
- having a partner who is consistent in the ways that they show up for you

## *Exercise: Building Emotional Safety in Your Relationship*

Emotional safety can be found when we intentionally choose to listen, when we are intentional with our body language, when we celebrate small wins, and when we are patient with each other. It takes a lot of work, but it will be worth it to know that your partner is at ease and that your presence feels like home.

- **Reflect on your own feelings:** Take a moment to think about how you feel in your relationship. Do you feel heard and understood? Do you feel safe sharing your thoughts and emotions with your partner? Write down your thoughts and feelings in a journal or diary.

- **Communicate your needs:** Talk to your partner about what you need in order to feel emotionally safe in the relationship. Be honest and direct, but also be willing to listen to their perspective. Use "I" statements, such as "I feel unsafe when…" or "I need…" rather than blaming or attacking language.

- **Practice active listening:** When your partner is speaking, give them your full attention. Avoid interrupting, and ask questions for clarification if needed. Reflect back on what you hear to show that you understand and validate their feelings.

- **Set boundaries:** Boundaries are essential for building emotional safety. Identify what your boundaries are and communicate them clearly to your partner. Respect their boundaries as well.

- **Be consistent:** Consistency is key to building trust in a relationship. Be reliable and follow through on your commitments. Show up for your partner in the ways they need you to.

- **Validate their emotions:** Validate your partner's emotions and experiences, even if you don't necessarily agree with them. Let them know that their feelings are valid and that you are there to support them.

- **Practice forgiveness:** Conflict is inevitable in any relationship. When conflicts arise, practice forgiveness and work toward resolution. Avoid holding grudges or bringing up past hurts.

- **Celebrate each other:** Make time to celebrate each other's successes and accomplishments. Show appreciation and gratitude for each other on a regular basis. Leave notes for each other in the house. Surprise each other with your favorite treats and things and say "thank you" and "I love you" more often.

## Self-Reflection Exercises

Self-awareness is a very big and important part of our relationships and how we show up for them. When you love yourself, you begin to see yourself in your fullness, in your power, and in your unlimited abundance. It also allows you to reflect on all of the areas where you might be falling short in your relationship. Take for example Gracelyn, a lovely lady I worked with a while back. She was kind, intelligent, ambitious, beautiful, and so full of life, but when it came to her romantic relationships, she seemed to struggle.

Through our discussions, she realized that she had a tendency to put other people's needs before her own, even when it meant compromising her own values and beliefs. She also found that she had a hard time communicating her needs and boundaries in her relationships, which often left her feeling resentful and unfulfilled. As she grew more self-aware, she began to take steps to address these issues. She started setting boundaries and communicating her needs more assertively with her partner. She also began to prioritize her own self-care and well-being, which helped her feel more confident and empowered in her relationships.

This self-awareness that she developed allowed her to take full responsibility for her own happiness and build healthier, more fulfilling relationships. She also realized that self-love and self-care are essential components of any successful relationship. When you love and respect yourself, you are better equipped to love and respect others and to show up as your best self in all your interactions because you can only meet where you are willing to meet yourself.

If you are working on finding out where that relationship with yourself is, here is a brief exercise that you can try:

1. Take a few deep breaths and allow yourself to relax.

2. Ask yourself, "How do I feel about myself?" Take a moment to tune into your thoughts, emotions, and sensations.

3. Write down the thoughts and feelings that come up without judgment or criticism. If you feel stuck, try asking yourself specific questions such as, "What do I like about myself?" or "What do I want to change?"

4. Once you have a list of your thoughts and feelings, try to identify any patterns or recurring themes. For example, you may notice that you have a lot of negative self-talk or that you struggle with self-doubt.

5. Next, ask yourself, "How do I want to feel about myself?" Write down your ideal thoughts and feelings, even if they seem out of reach.

6. Compare your current thoughts and feelings to your ideal ones. Identify any gaps or areas where you would like to improve.

7. Finally, brainstorm some concrete actions you can take to bridge the gap between where you are and where you want to be. For example, you might commit to practicing self-compassion, setting boundaries, or pursuing a hobby that brings you joy.

Remember, this exercise is not about judging yourself or trying to be perfect. It's about gaining awareness and taking intentional steps toward a healthier and more fulfilling relationship with yourself.

## Claim Your Free Self-Care Bonus: A Gift Just for You!

*I am deeply committed to offering you more than just words on a page. That's why, throughout this book, I've included a series of specially crafted bonuses to add depth to your journey and support you even further along the path you're walking. Think of these as moments of pause, designed to help you nurture yourself as you navigate each chapter. You can download each bonus whenever you feel called to dive deeper—right away, or whenever the time feels right.*

*If you agree that self-care is essential to nurturing your relationship, take the next step with* **my Nurturing Self-Care Guide**, *available to you as a free download. Head to* https://booksforbetterlife.com/relationship-workbook *or simply scan the QR code.*

*This guide is a personal collection of my go-to tools: calming meditations, grounding yoga poses, and my favorite self-care routines. Each element is crafted to help you reconnect, recharge, and reclaim a moment just for you. Don't wait—these moments are yours to embrace. You deserve this.*

*I truly believe in the power of sharing, and I'm convinced that these free bonuses will be invaluable in guiding you forward!*

WEEK 1: FOUNDATIONS OF CONNECTION

# Establishing Open Communication Channels

Communication is attractive, sexy, and something that will never grow old in relationships. It's the kind of thing that bridges gaps in relationships. It tells the person who you are with that they matter enough to you that you are willing to make that sacrifice and the effort to try and make the relationship work. It's in the small things:

- How can I support you today?
- Are you feeling seen, heard, and understood?
- When do you feel most loved?
- Are there any insecurities that you feel about us?
- I felt upset when you said (insert). Can we talk about that?
- How are you really doing? How was your day? That's when you really listen.

Some conversations will never be easy to have, and some questions will never be easy to ask, but when we avoid that short-term discomfort, we trade it in for something that is much more sinister: long-term dysfunction. When we decide not to have a difficult conversation, we forget that we are, in fact, making an active choice not to do so. We are choosing long-term discomfort, guilt, and the awkwardness of speaking our own truth.

When I am struggling with the process of speaking my own truth, I stop and ask myself how I will feel a day, a week, or a year from now.

If I choose not to speak up, I imagine myself lying sleeplessly in my bed, nursing resentment like an infant, and finding ways to avoid that particular person or situation in question. I see myself spending so much unnecessary energy constructing my whole life around the difficulty, and then one year later, finding myself in the same position: stuck, silent, and resentful.

But if I make the conscious choice to speak up, even if it scares me, I imagine myself soldiering on through that tough conversation, yes, feeling awkward afterward, but falling asleep so peacefully afterward and eventually finding new ways to relate to that person. I see myself telling myself how proud I am of myself, and one year later, looking back at the conversation in question, it is a distant memory because I handled it with integrity.

I won't go too deeply into detail about how important communication is and so forth because we're going discuss it at a later stage, but what I will say, and what I want you to remember, is that honest communication leaves enough room for us to be able to breathe in our relationships.

## Identifying and Expressing Individual Needs

Being able to express your individual needs to your partner is essential in building a healthy and fulfilling relationship. When you are open and honest about your needs, it helps to create a safe environment for both you and your partner to communicate and work together toward meeting each other's needs.

When we keep our needs hidden, we are indirectly telling our partner that their needs are more important than ours. This can lead to resentment and frustration, which can cause a rift in the relationship. On the other hand, when we express our needs, we are allowing our partner to understand us better, and this can help to build intimacy and strengthen the relationship. It's also important to keep in mind that expressing needs is not a one-time thing. Our needs can change over time, and it's important to continue to express them as they change. By doing so, we can ensure that both partners feel heard, respected, and valued in the relationship.

**Here's an exercise I want you to try:**

Kate and Mark have been dating for a little over two and a half years and have just moved in together. While they were excited about this new chapter in their relationship, they were also nervous about how they would navigate their different needs and expectations in this new living arrangement. To help them communicate their needs effectively, they decided to do an exercise together. They sat down with a piece of paper and a pen and wrote out a scenario where one of them had a need that the other wasn't aware of.

They then took turns sharing their scenarios and discussing how they would communicate their needs to their partner. Kate went first. She wrote down that she sometimes struggled with anxiety and needed alone time to recharge. She shared with Mark that sometimes, when she's feeling overwhelmed, she needs to retreat to a quiet space and be alone for a while. She expressed how important it was for her to have this time and asked Mark to respect her need for space. Mark listened attentively and then shared his own scenario. He wrote down that he sometimes felt stressed and needed help with household chores. He explained to Kate that when he was feeling overwhelmed, he needed her to step in and help out more with things like cooking and cleaning. He asked her to be more proactive in offering to help out when he was feeling stressed.

After they had both shared their scenarios, they took some time to reflect on what they had learned about each other. They realized that they had been making assumptions about each other's needs without actually communicating them. They also realized that by sharing their needs, they were able to deepen their understanding of each other and strengthen their relationship. To continue making this a normal part of their relationship, they decided to make it a regular part of their conversations. They committed to checking in with each other regularly and asking how they could better support each other's needs.

You aren't needy for having needs in your relationship, just like your partner isn't either; that's why you need to learn how to find a middle ground for both.

Here's a step-by-step guide to how you and your partner will both learn to communicate your individual needs:

## Step 1: Take some time for self-reflection

The first step in identifying your individual needs in a relationship is to take some time for self-reflection. Ask yourself, "What do I need to feel fulfilled and happy in my relationship?" Take some time to think about your personal values, beliefs, and priorities. This will help you to identify what is most important to you in a relationship.

## Step 2: Make a list of your needs

Once you have reflected on what is important to you, make a list of your needs. Be specific and clear about what you need from your partner to feel fulfilled in the relationship. Your needs could be emotional, physical, or practical. For example, you might need your partner to listen to you when you're feeling upset, spend quality time with you, or help out more around the house.

## Step 3: Prioritize your needs

After you have made a list of your needs, prioritize them. Which needs are essential for your happiness and well-being, and which ones are less important? This will help you to communicate your needs to your partner more effectively and ensure that they understand which ones are most important to you.

## Step 4: Consider your partner's needs

Remember that a relationship is a two-way street. Consider your partner's needs as well and think about how they can be met in a way that is mutually beneficial. This will help to create a healthy and fulfilling relationship where both partners feel valued and respected.

## Step 5: Practice expressing your needs

Now that you have identified your needs, it's time to practice expressing them to your partner. Start by sharing one or two of your most important needs with your partner. Be clear and specific about what you need and why it's important to you. Ask your partner to listen to you and respond in a nonjudgmental and supportive way.

## Step 6: Reflect on your communication

After you have expressed your needs, take some time to reflect on how the conversation went. Did you feel heard and understood? Did your partner respond in a supportive way? If not, think about how you can communicate your needs more effectively and try again.

## Step 7: Continue to communicate your needs

Remember that expressing your needs is something that you have to do consistently if you want to get better at it. As your relationship evolves, your needs may change, so it's important to continue to communicate them with your partner. Regular check-ins can help ensure that both partners feel heard and valued in the relationship.

Love is deeply layered. At its core, it is about deep care, and with that can sometimes come complex kinds of emotions that are, at times, incredibly tricky. The relationships that matter most to us will always be worth those difficult conversations, the effort to fix things, and the deep care that says, "You matter to me." Communication is going where love resides and making the deliberate choice to stay.

## Notes

# Week 2: Effective Communication

*"Communication works for those who work at it."*

— JOHN POWELL

Knowing that we are not responsible for other people's bad moods, silent treatment, negative reactions toward our boundaries, lack of emotional maturity, or victim mentality is true growth. Our behaviors are an indication of our own inner work that still needs to be done, and other people's behaviors are an indication of their work.

Communication is an essential aspect of any successful relationship. It is the foundation upon which trust, understanding, and love are built. Without communication, relationships are bound to fail, leaving one partner feeling neglected and unimportant. The story of the guy who taught me about breadcrumbing is a perfect example of how communication plays a vital role in a relationship.

When I was dating this guy, I thought I was in love, but in reality, I was just chasing after someone who was not interested in me. I found myself begging for scraps of his attention, and even when I got it, it was never enough. He would give just enough to keep me at bay but never enough to make me feel valued. I was left feeling unimportant and unloved, and eventually, the relationship ended.

What I learned from that experience is that in a relationship, it's not enough to just be physically present. You have to be emotionally present, too. You have to communicate your feelings, your thoughts, and your desires. If you don't, the other person will feel neglected, and the relationship will start to crumble.

Effective communication is not just about talking; it's also about listening. It's about being present in the moment and actively listening to what the other person is saying. It's about being empathetic and understanding their perspective. Communication is also about being honest and transparent. If something is bothering you, don't keep it inside. Talk about it with your partner, and together, find a solution that works for both of you.

Patience plays an important part in it, too. Sometimes, it takes time for people to open up and share their feelings. It's okay to give them space and time to process their emotions. It does take a while to get to that place where you are able to articulate your emotions well enough.

## Openness and Honesty in Relationships

Honesty is saying what is true, but wisdom is knowing the right way to say it.

Let's say that your partner has a habit of leaving their clothes on the floor instead of putting them in the hamper. This habit annoys you, but you're not sure how to bring it up without causing an argument. Instead of letting your frustration build up, take some time to think about why this habit bothers you. Perhaps you feel like your partner is not respecting your shared living space, or maybe you're worried that the mess will attract bugs or create an unpleasant smell. Once you have a clear understanding of your feelings, choose a time when you and your partner are both relaxed and not distracted.

Start the conversation by expressing your love and appreciation for your partner, and then calmly and respectfully share your feelings about the clothes on the floor. For example, you could say something like, "Hey, I just wanted to talk to you about something that's been on my mind. I love you, and I appreciate all that you do, but I've been feeling frustrated lately when I see clothes on the floor instead of in the hamper. It makes me feel like our living space isn't as clean and organized as we both want it to be, and I'm worried that it could attract bugs or create an unpleasant smell. I wanted to bring it up because I value honesty and openness in our relationship, and I think that by talking about it, we can find a solution that works for both of us."

When you approach the situation with kindness and understanding, you're more likely to have a productive conversation and find a solution that works for both of you. Your partner may not even realize that their habit is bothering you, and by bringing it up in a nonjudgmental way, you can work together to create a living space that feels comfortable and clean for both of you.

## Nurturing a Safe Space for communication

- **Trust and vulnerability**: Let your walls come down, open up the curtains, and allow everything to flow through the good and the bad, the scary and the in-between. Allow yourself and your partner to be vulnerable with each other. This means creating an environment where it's safe to share fears. Basically, use statements like 'I understand" and "I hear you." Try to stay away from language that would make it seem like you are judging them, their insecurities, and past experiences.

- **Active listening:** Don't listen to respond; listen to understand. Take the time to truly listen to your partner. Allow their words to sink in and soak right through you. Let empathy lead you and try to understand their perspective without immediately formulating a response.

- **Openness and honesty:** Encourage openness and honesty in your communication. This means being transparent and authentic with each other, even if it's uncomfortable at times.

- **Respect and support:** Your partner feels what they feel, and you feel what you feel, so there should be no reason to shame or ridicule them for what they are feeling.

- **Love and understanding:** Where love leads, there will always be a way. There will always be a sliver of light. Approach your communication with love and understanding. Remember that you're a team, and your goal is to understand each other better and strengthen your connection.

## Active Listening Techniques

Most of us actually aren't good listeners at all. We hear people when they're talking to us, but we don't understand them all that well. We're selectively filtering out the important things and interpreting them in a way that we want. For example, if your partner tells you that they are tired, you'll interpret that perhaps as a message that they don't want to actually spend time with you when, in all actuality, the underlying message is simply just, "Honey, I'm empty, and there is not much of me that I can give to you right now."

It's crucial to realize that in such a moment, there is more than just an exchange of words happening—it's a complex dance of emotions, unspoken needs, and a plea for understanding. When your others say they're tired, we might only hear a statement of physical exhaustion. But beneath the surface, there's a subtext playing a tune that's often missed.

It's like they're handing you an invisible gift, one that requires you to peel back the layers of what's unsaid to reveal the true sentiment behind their words. They're not just notifying you of their need to rest; they're inviting you into their inner world, a place where vulnerability resides and the unspoken truth echoes loudly.

True listening, in that case, becomes an art form, a skill that is honed over time with patience and genuine care. It involves an open heart and an attentive mind. It's about being fully present in the moment without the distraction of your own thoughts, judgments, or the buzz of your surroundings. It's about creating a sacred space where your partner feels seen, heard, and valued.

Imagine you're a sculptor, and every word your partner utters is a block of marble. Your task is not to chip away at the block with your own interpretations or solutions but to carefully observe the shape that's emerging. You're there to understand the contours of their feelings and the textures of their needs. When your partner says they're tired, maybe the marble reveals a figure weighed down by the day's burdens, seeking not solutions but simply a space to be acknowledged.

It means, "I am here. My attention and focus are on you and your words." This statement isn't just a casual remark but rather a powerful affirmation of your presence. It's you saying that, in this moment, nothing else is as important as their thoughts and emotions. It's you offering a gift of your time and attention, which, in the currency of relationships, is priceless.

Listening is about empathy, to mentally and emotionally walk in your partner's shoes. It's about resisting the urge to interrupt with your own narrative or to fix things hastily. Instead, active listening involves a delicate balance of silence, affirmation, and feedback that encourages further sharing. It's about using verbal and nonverbal cues to show you're engaged—nodding your head, maintaining eye contact, and perhaps most importantly, mirroring back what you've heard to confirm your understanding.

In doing so, you're not only validating their experience but also reinforcing the bond of trust and intimacy that is so vital in any relationship. You're signaling that, no matter how mundane or profound the topic, you're there to support and to understand. It's this level of attentive listening that can transform simple conversations into bridges of connection, helping to weave the fabric of a stronger, more resilient partnership.

## Practicing Active Listening

It's funny how a slight misinterpretation of words can lead to frustration in our relationships, so many of us also often assume that our partners have been with us for however long, so they must know what we are thinking and feeling. But the truth is that communication is key in any relationship, and active listening is a crucial part of that.

Active listening is not just about hearing the words that are being said, but it's about truly understanding what your partner was feeling in that moment. It involves bringing your whole self to the conversation, showing that you are genuinely interested in what they have to say; it's about putting aside your own biases for a moment and really focusing on your partner.

So, how can we practice active listening in our relationships? Here are a few exercises that can help improve your active listening skills:

- **The mirror exercise:** Sit facing your partner and take turns speaking for a few minutes while the other person simply mirrors back what they heard. This means repeating what your partner said in your own words. This exercise helps ensure that you are truly understanding what your partner is saying and gives them the opportunity to clarify if there are any misunderstandings.

- **The five-second pause:** When your partner finishes speaking, take a five-second pause before responding. This gives you a moment to fully process what they said and formulate a thoughtful response. It also shows your partner that you are not just waiting for your turn to speak but that you are actively listening to them.

- **Nonverbal cues:** Pay attention to your nonverbal cues when your partner is speaking. Make eye contact, nod your head, and use encouraging gestures to show that you are engaged in the conversation.

This can help your partner feel heard and understood.

- **Ask open-ended questions:** Instead of just waiting for your turn to talk, ask your partner open-ended questions that encourage them to expand on their thoughts and feelings. This shows that you are genuinely interested in what they have to say and want to understand them better.

- **Reflective listening:** Practice reflective listening by summarizing what your partner said and reflecting it back to them. For example, this might sound like, "Oh, so basically, when I did (insert scenario), it made you feel unseen, unheard, and unimportant, and you might have interpreted that as me having little to no regard for your opinion." This not only shows that you were actively listening, but it also gives your partner the opportunity to clarify or expand on their thoughts.

## Nonviolent Communication

My grandmother and my grandfather were married for 60 years. I remember that there were many, many occasions to ask her, "How did you make it work for so long?" She simply just smiled, one day, her answer came completely unexpected, "A harsh word uttered is like throwing a stone in a hornet's nest, so even in anger, let love lead the way. Let it hold you steady until you find the right words to say without hurting the one you love dearly."

I was taken aback by her response. It was a profound statement, and I could sense that it had come from a place of experience. She went on to share a story from early in her marriage that had taught her the importance of non-confrontational communication. She recounted an incident where my grandfather had come home late from work without informing her. She had been worried sick and was furious when he finally came home. She had wanted to lash out at him, but something held her back. She took a deep breath and decided to use a different approach. Instead of confronting him, she calmly asked him where he had been and why he had not called.

Though he was initially defensive, her non-confrontational approach made him more open to communicating. He explained that he had been caught up in a meeting and had lost track of time. My grandmother's non-confrontational approach allowed my grandfather to feel heard and understood. It had also prevented a potential argument that could have escalated into something bigger. From that day forward, she knew she had to make a conscious effort to communicate in a non-confrontational way, even when she was angry or upset. She had come to realize that it was possible to communicate effectively without hurting the ones you love. I realized as I listened to her story, that non-confrontational communication was not just about avoiding conflict. It was about being mindful of the impact of our words and actions on others, especially those we love. This approach of hers allowed her to express her feelings while also respecting my grandfather's perspective. I realized that this approach she recommended was not just relevant to romantic relationships but could be applied to all types of relationships. The importance of non-confrontational communication cannot be overstated, and my grandmother's wisdom has given me a newfound appreciation for this approach.

We rarely think about the impact our words will have on the other person once they are uttered. At that moment, we are usually just thinking about ourselves, our hurt, and the consequences. *"You never listen to anything I say.", "You always do x, y, z.", "You don't care about me as much as you say you do."* Do any of these sound familiar?

Confrontational communication is an aggressive approach to communication that often leads to conflicts and misunderstandings. When we communicate confrontationally, we tend to use language that is harsh, critical, and accusatory. We may also use body language, like eye-rolling or crossed arms, that can be perceived as hostile or defensive.

Confrontational communication can be damaging to our relationships because it makes our partners feel attacked or criticized. When we communicate confrontationally, we put the other person on the defensive, which can lead to a breakdown in communication. As a result, conflicts can escalate, and relationships can suffer.

One of the other biggest problems with it is that it often leads to a cycle of blame. When we communicate confrontationally, we tend to focus on what the other person has done wrong instead of finding a solution to the problem. This can lead to a situation where both parties are blaming each other, and no progress is being made.

It is also a sign of underlying issues in the relationship. When we communicate confrontationally, we may be expressing our frustration or anger about something that is not related to the current situation. For example, if we are upset about our partner's lack of attention, we may start a fight about something unrelated, like leaving the toilet seat up.

Non-confrontational communication, on the other hand, is a more effective, gentler, and kinder approach to communication. It involves using language that is respectful, nonjudgmental, and empathetic. With non-confrontational communication, we can express our feelings and concerns without attacking the other person. It is not about avoiding conflict. Instead, it is about finding a way to communicate effectively without hurting the other person. When we communicate non-confrontationally, we can listen to the other person's perspective and work together to find a solution to the problem.

Non-confrontational communication sounds a little like:

- *"I noticed that you haven't been spending as much time with me lately. Is everything okay?"*

- *"I feel hurt when you cancel plans at the last minute. Can we talk about how we can avoid this in the future?"*

- *"I'm feeling overwhelmed with the workload lately. Can we work together to figure out a solution?"*

- *"I appreciate your help, but I would prefer if you could ask me before making decisions on my behalf."*

- *"I really value spending time with you, but I also need some alone time to recharge. Can we find a balance that works for both of us?"*

- *"I understand that you have a different opinion, but I would like to share my perspective as well."*

- *"I'm sorry if I came across as dismissive earlier. Can we revisit that topic and discuss it further?*

- *I feel like we're not on the same page about this. Can we take some time to clarify our understanding of the issue?"*

- *"I understand that you're upset, but I would appreciate it if you could communicate in a way that is respectful and constructive."*

- *"I really value our relationship, and I want to work together to find a solution that works for both of us."*

When we communicate, we often unconsciously bring our own emotional baggage and past experiences into the conversation. This can lead to misunderstandings and conflicts, especially when we communicate confrontationally. One way to become a non-confrontational communicator is to address and unpack our own emotional wounds. Our emotional wounds can manifest in the language that we use, the tone of our voice, our body language, and even our facial expressions. For example, if we have experienced abandonment in the past, we may feel triggered when our partner is late to meet us and say something like, "You don't care about me as much as you say you do." This statement may not accurately reflect the situation, but it reflects our own unresolved trauma.

Another thing that we can do is to learn to wear empathy like a second skin. Here's the reality: All of us, in some way or another, are a little hard to love. We all suffer from something, so when you meet someone who is willing to stay committed to understanding you and actually wants to grow with you, don't let your pride and stubbornness ruin it. This means putting ourselves in the other person's shoes and trying to understand their perspective. We can also validate their feelings, even if we don't agree with them. For example, we can say, *"I understand that you're feeling hurt, and I'm sorry that I contributed to that."*

You can also learn to say what you are seeing, but then also check out what it is that you're saying. For this to work, you will have to open your heart up to the possibility that your view might change. You are basically inviting them to understand what it is that you're seeing. It's about not jumping to conclusions before you get the full picture of what's going on.

## Conflict Resolution

Okay, so small and big fights between you and your partner are inevitable. You guys are going to have things that you disagree on, and when that happens, you're going to need to know how to resolve and fix the problem so that you guys get to a place where you're all okay again.

**Here's how you can do that:**

You create a welcoming and open environment. People shut down when they feel like they are being attacked. In healthy relationships, you and your partner are able to voice what is on your heart without fearing that you will be judged and whatnot. It's important to talk about not only the things that are on our hearts but also the things that are going well—the things that our partners are doing well. If you feel like you cannot talk about things like money or the big picture, things that scare and mean something to you, that relationship may be unhealthy. If you cannot express your feelings without the fear of retaliation, then something is amiss.

Keep calm and be respectful. Don't cross lines and hurl insults at your partner or say things that you know they will not take too well. Keep the focus on the dispute at hand, and don't bring unnecessary personal jibes into it. Regardless of what caused the argument, there shouldn't be attacks or anything that might make your partner angrier.

Look at the root cause of the problem. Sometimes, when we argue with our partners, it's because there are certain needs of ours that aren't being met. If it feels to you like your partner is sweating the small stuff, take a moment to evaluate whether there is a larger issue at hand. For instance, if your partner is upset that they are not spending that much time with you, they might simply want you to find a little more balance. Consider things from their point of view; if things were reversed, how would you feel? Be understanding instead of just trying to push your point across.

Be careful of those arguments that start because there's a need for control. No one should be controlled, especially by a partner. This is a major red flag in relationships. Our partners aren't our property; they are their own people with lives of their own. So, exhibiting controlling behavior and blaming it on the fact that we love them is just outrightly being manipulative.

Choose your battles. Sometimes, we just need to agree to disagree. It's called compromise. Are you guys arguing over dinner or what Netflix show you should be watching next? If you pause and think to yourself, *I won't be mad about this next week*, then it's just best to let it go. You and your partner are not going to agree on absolutely everything, so if you feel that the issue is too big, maybe you should contemplate if you are compatible.

## WEEK 2: EFFECTIVE COMMUNICATION

**Let's see what these tips would look like in practice:**

Okay, so you and your partner have a household chores roster to help split up the tasks in the house and make them easier to manage for everyone. However, you find that your partner is not following through on their share of the chores, and it's starting to create tension between you both. Here's an exercise you can try to put the conflict resolution tips into practice:

- **Create a safe and welcoming environment**: Set aside time to talk to your partner about the issue that's bothering you. Make sure that you both have the time and space to talk without distractions or interruptions.

- **Keep calm and be respectful**: When talking to your partner, keep the focus on the issue at hand and avoid personal attacks or insults. Use *"I"* statements instead of *"you"* statements to express your feelings. For example, *"I feel hurt when you do or say x, y, z,"* or *"I would appreciate it if you consulted me over (insert topic)."*

- **Get to the root cause of the problem**: Try to understand why your partner is not following through on their share of the chores. Is there a larger issue at hand? Are they feeling overwhelmed or stressed? Listen to their point of view and try to find a solution that works for both of you.

- **Be careful of controlling behavior**: Avoid making demands or ultimatums and remember that your partner is their own person and has the right to make their own decisions.

- **Choose your battles**: Decide which issues are worth fighting over and which ones you can let go. In this case, the issue of household chores may be important to you, but it may not be worth jeopardizing your relationship over. Find a compromise that works for both of you, such as revisiting the chores roster and adjusting it to fit your schedules and responsibilities better.

## Things to Remember About Conflict

Conflict can make it feel as if our relationships are falling apart, but that is not the case. It's a natural part of relationships. Here are a few things to remember:

- **Just because you and your partner have a conflict, it does not mean that your relationship is failing.** Conflict is a normal part of any relationship, and it's how you handle it that really matters.

- **Remember that you and your partner are on the same team.** When you're in conflict, it's easy to feel like you're against each other, but it's important to remember that you both want the same thing: a strong and healthy relationship.

- **Conflict can be an opportunity for growth.** When you work through conflict together, you learn more about each other and what makes your relationship work. This can make your bond even stronger in the long run.

- **Communication is key**. When you're in conflict, it's important to communicate openly and honestly with your partner. This means listening to their perspective as well as expressing your own.

- **Don't be afraid to take a break.** Sometimes, when emotions are running high, it's best to take a break from the conflict and come back to it later when you're both feeling more level-headed.

- **Remember that compromise is not a bad thing.** In fact, compromise is often the best solution when it comes to resolving conflict. It's about finding a solution that works for both of you, not just one person.

- **Conflict can be an opportunity to practice empathy.** When you're in conflict, try to put yourself in your partner's shoes and see things from their perspective. This can help you understand their point of view and find a solution that works for both of you.

- **It's okay to ask for help.** If you're really struggling with conflict in your relationship, it's okay to seek the help of a therapist or counselor. They can provide you with the tools and support you need to navigate the conflict in a healthy way.

- **Remember that conflict does not define your relationship.** It's easy to get caught up in the moment and feel like your entire relationship is falling apart, but it's important to remember that conflict is just one part of your journey together.

- **Don't give up.** Conflict can be tough, but don't give up on your relationship. Keep working through things together, and remember that with time and effort, you can overcome any obstacle.

## *Notes on Compromise*

Compromise is very much a big part of loving and being loved, so here are a few notes from my heart that I'd like for you to keep etched onto your heart:

- **Start by understanding each other's needs:** Take the time to listen to your partner's perspective and understand their needs and concerns. This will help you find a solution that works for both of you.

- **Look for common ground:** Find areas where you both agree and build from there. This can help you find a compromise that works for both of you.

- **Be willing to give a little:** Compromise involves both parties making concessions. Be willing to give a little to get a little. This can help build trust and strengthen your relationship.

- **Stay open-minded:** Be willing to consider new ideas and solutions. Sometimes, the best compromise is one that neither of you had considered before.

- **Stay focused on the issue at hand:** When you're in conflict, it's easy to get sidetracked by personal attacks and other issues. Stay focused on the issue at hand and work together to find a solution.

- **Be patient:** Compromise takes time and effort. Be patient with each other, and don't give up if you don't find a solution right away.

- **Be respectful:** Respect each other's opinions and feelings. Avoid personal attacks and insults. This will help create a safe and welcoming environment for compromise.

- **Keep the big picture in mind:** When you're in conflict, it's easy to get caught up in the moment. Keep the big picture in mind and remember why you're in this relationship in the first place.

- **Don't be afraid to revisit the compromise:** If the compromise you come up with isn't working, don't be afraid to revisit it and make adjustments. Relationships are a work in progress, and compromise is an ongoing process too.

- **Celebrate the tiny victories:** When you come to a compromise that works for both of you, take the time to celebrate your success. This will help build positivity and strengthen your bond.

# WEEK 2: EFFECTIVE COMMUNICATION

## Notes

# Week 3: Understanding Your Love Language

*"I'll be loving you, always with a love that is true."*

— PATSY CLINE

*Dear self,* writes a hopeful 21-year-old me.

*You deserve soft love. A love that holds you gently and speaks tenderly to your little heart. You deserve a love that listens and remembers the tiny little things about you. The little things that you mention in passing are the ones that matter the most. They show that someone is paying attention to you, that they care about you, and that they want to make you happy.*

*You deserve someone in your life who sees you for who you truly are and loves you unconditionally. Someone who accepts your flaws and imperfections and still thinks you're amazing. Someone who makes you feel safe and secure and who you can trust with your deepest fears and vulnerabilities. This kind of love is not always easy to find, but it's out there. And when you do find it, hold onto it tightly and cherish it. Nurture it, grow it, and let it fill your heart with joy and happiness.*

# WEEK 3: UNDERSTANDING YOUR LOVE LANGUAGE

*May you also remember, too, that love is not just a feeling; it's also a choice. It's a choice to show up for someone every day, to support them, to encourage them, and to be there for them no matter what. It's a choice to prioritize their happiness and well-being over your own.*

*So, dear self, when you find someone like this in your life who loves you in this way, be grateful for them. Thank them for all the little things they do that make your life brighter. I know you haven't found them yet, but I know they're on the way. Keep your heart open and trust that it will come to you when the time is right.*

*Loves, Me*

This was a hopeful and romantic version of me who penned this letter. It's idealistic, but this young me sure knew what she wanted. As I read this letter, one sentence stands out to me: *"A love that holds you gently and speaks tenderly to your little heart."* It's a beautiful sentiment, but it's also a reflection of my love language at the time—physical touch.

As I've grown older, though, I've come to realize that my love languages are not just limited to physical touch but also words of affirmation, quality time, acts of service, and receiving gifts. In fact, reading this letter has made me realize how important it is to understand our own love languages and those of the people we love. It's not enough to just love someone, we need to love them in a way that they feel loved and appreciated.

I mean, think about it: If my partner's love language is words of affirmation, telling them how much I love and appreciate them on a regular basis would mean the world to them. If their love language is acts of service, doing something for them, like cooking them a meal or helping them with a task, would make them feel loved and valued.

We base our relationships on assumptions at times, but It's also important to remember that we can't assume that our partners have the same love language as us. Sometimes, we may love someone in a way that we want to be loved, but it may not necessarily be how they want to be loved.

Reading this letter again has reminded me why having a voice in a relationship is important, and also having ears that are open enough to listen. By communicating our love languages and taking the time to understand each other's needs and desires, we can build a stronger, more fulfilling relationship.

Love languages are a gateway, a map to love. They are the keys that unlock the intricacies of human connection, allowing us to express and receive love in the ways that resonate most deeply with our hearts. Just as each person is unique, so too are their love languages, reflecting the beautiful diversity of human emotion and experience.

Words of affirmation, one of the five love languages, are like gentle whispers of love that wrap around the soul, nurturing it with positivity and encouragement. A simple, heartfelt "I love you," or a sincere acknowledgment of someone's efforts can speak volumes, affirming their worth and kindling the fires of affection within their heart. Through the power of uplifting words, we can build bridges of connection and strengthen the bonds of love.

Acts of service, another love language, are the silent symphonies of love that resonate through selfless deeds and thoughtful gestures. From preparing a favorite meal to offering a helping hand in times of need, these acts speak loudly of love, demonstrating care and consideration in ways that transcend words. They show that love is not just something we feel but something we do, weaving the fabric of our lives with threads of kindness and devotion.

Gifts, as a love language, are tangible expressions of affection, each one a treasure chest of emotions waiting to be unwrapped. Whether grand or humble, a gift speaks the language of love, saying, "I see you, I cherish you, and I hold you close to my heart." It's not the material value that matters but the sentiment behind the gift—the thought and love woven into its very essence.

Quality time, a love language that speaks through undivided attention and meaningful togetherness, forms the canvas upon which cherished memories are painted. When we offer our presence and our time, we offer a piece of ourselves, creating a shared sanctuary where love can flourish and grow. In a world filled with distractions, the act of carving out time for one another is a testament to the depth of our love and the value we place on our relationships.

Physical touch, the final love language, is the language of connection, speaking volumes through a gentle caress, a warm embrace, or a reassuring hand on the shoulder. It's a language that transcends barriers, expressing love in its most primal and profound form. Through touch, we communicate a myriad of emotions—comfort, passion, reassurance, and so much more—weaving an intricate tapestry of love with every gentle touch.

Understanding and embracing these love languages is crucial for fostering healthy, fulfilling relationships. By recognizing and speaking our partner's love language, we demonstrate that we see and value them for who they are, nurturing a deep sense of connection and intimacy. Moreover, by articulating our own love language, we provide our loved ones with the guidance they need to express their love in ways that truly resonate with us, fostering mutual understanding and harmony within our relationships.

# What's Your Love Language?

Here is a sample questionnaire for couples to figure out their love languages together. Give each question a mark, on a scale of 1 to 10, and see at the end for which love language you score the most points:

**Words of Affirmation:**

- When I express my love, I often use words of encouragement and praise.
- I feel loved when my partner compliments me or expresses appreciation for something I've done.
- I value verbal affirmations as a way to feel loved and appreciated.

**Acts of Service:**

- I feel loved when my partner does things for me without me having to ask.
- I express my love by doing helpful things for my partner, such as cooking a meal or running errands.
- I value when my partner helps me with tasks or chores as a way to feel loved and cared for.

**Receiving Gifts:**

- I feel loved when my partner gives me thoughtful gifts or surprises.
- I express my love by giving gifts or tokens of appreciation to my partner.
- I value when my partner gives me meaningful gifts as a way to feel loved and valued.

**Quality Time:**

- I feel loved when my partner spends uninterrupted time with me, giving me their full attention.
- I express my love by making an effort to spend quality time with my partner, such as going on dates or having meaningful conversations.
- I value when my partner prioritizes spending time with me as a way to feel loved and connected.

**Physical Touch:**

- I feel loved when my partner shows affection through physical touch, such as holding hands, hugging, or kissing.
- I express my love through physical affection and enjoy being close to my partner.
- I value physical touch as a way to feel loved and emotionally connected.

After completing the questionnaire, you can interpret the results by discussing your individual love languages with each other. You can compare answers and see which love languages you have in common and which ones are different. This can help you understand how you each prefer to give and receive love and how you can better meet each other's emotional needs in the relationship. It can also open up a dialogue about how you can express love in ways that resonate with your partner's love language.

Also, remember that it's okay if you find that you have more than one love language. Most people usually have a combination of several of these.

So, a while back, I dated this guy who would, without fail, make me a morning cup of coffee, just as I liked it. This would seem completely normal to someone else, but to me, it meant the world. It was his way of showing me love through acts of service, which I later realized was his primary love language. This simple gesture of making my coffee every morning made me feel cared for and appreciated in a way that words could never fully express.

The orange peel theory, in relation to love languages, is a concept that suggests that just like an orange, each person has their own unique way of expressing and receiving love. Just as the orange peel protects and conceals the fruit inside, our love languages can sometimes be hidden or not fully understood by our partners. By taking the time to understand and appreciate each other's love languages, we can peel back the layers and truly connect on a deeper level.

Understanding and honoring each other's love languages can lead to a more fulfilling and harmonious relationship. It allows us to communicate love in a way that resonates with our partner, leading to a deeper emotional connection and a stronger bond. Just like the orange peel theory, when we take the time to understand and appreciate each other's unique way of expressing and receiving love, we can create a more loving and nurturing relationship.

## Incorporating Love Languages Into Daily Interactions

Love is a choice. We wake up and make the conscious effort to love the people who we are with, shortcomings and all. I have learned that we will only ever be able to love people with this kind of selflessness when we learn to meet ourselves where we are.

- **Communicate openly:** Discuss each other's love languages and how you can best fulfill each other's emotional needs. For example, you can say something along the lines of it would make me feel so loved if you got me flowers every now and again without me asking.

- **Practice active listening:** You are not going to learn more about your partner and their needs if you aren't making an intentional choice to find out what it is that they like and what they don't like. Pay attention to their preferences and make a conscious effort to speak their love language.

- **Show appreciation:** I think so often, when we get comfortable with people doing stuff for us, we forget to thank them for the little things. Express gratitude and acknowledge their partner's efforts in their love language, whether it's through words of affirmation, acts of service, or quality time. Thank you for spending time with me today. Thank you for the coffee or the tea. Thank you for being you. It seems so insignificant, but believe me, it makes a big difference.

- **Be intentional:** If you say that you are going to do something, do it, and don't just flake out on them. Make a conscious effort to incorporate their love language into everyday interactions, whether it's a small act of kindness or a meaningful conversation. Love does take work; we can't expect it to be all smooth sailing all the time, but wherever we can, we can work on making things significantly easier.

- **Plan activities:** Make time for each other and prioritize that connection that you have with them. Schedule activities or dates that cater to each other's love languages, such as a movie night for quality time or a surprise gift for receiving gifts.

- **Be empathetic:** People will like the things that they like, and a little further down the line, they might realize that they don't really like those things that much anymore. Understand that your partner's love language may be different from yours, and make an effort to appreciate and reciprocate their expressions of love Also, keep it at the back of your mind that their preferences might change in the long run as well.

- **Reassess and adapt:** As individuals grow and change, so too can their love languages. Have those times when you check in with one another to see that you are meeting each other's evolving emotional needs.

## Small Gestures of Love

Below you can discover some ways in which you can show your love to your partner for each love language.

**Words of Affirmation:**

- Leave a note of encouragement for your partner to find.
- Send a heartfelt text message expressing appreciation and love.
- Compliment your partner on their appearance or a job well done.

- Write a love letter or a poem for your partner.
- Verbally express your appreciation for something your partner has done.
- Tell your partner, "I love you" and "I'm proud of you" regularly.

**Acts of Service:**

- Take on a chore or task your partner usually handles.
- Make your partner's favorite meal without being asked.
- Fill up your partner's gas tank or get their car washed.
- Offer to run errands for your partner.
- Give your partner a massage after a long day.
- Assist your partner with a project or task they're working on.

**Receiving Gifts:**

- Bring home a small surprise or token of affection.
- Gift your partner their favorite snack or treat.
- Find a meaningful trinket or souvenir for your partner during your travels.
- Create a DIY gift or craft for your partner.
- Buy a book or item your partner has been wanting.
- Surprise your partner with a bouquet of flowers or a plant.

**Quality Time:**

- Plan a movie or game night together.
- Go for a walk or hike as a couple.
- Have a technology-free evening to focus solely on each other.
- Take a day trip or weekend getaway together.
- Schedule a regular date night.
- Have a deep conversation and actively listen to your partner.

**Physical Touch:**

- Hold hands while walking or sitting together.
- Hug your partner when they least expect it.
- Offer a comforting touch when your partner is upset.
- Cuddle on the couch while watching TV or reading.
- Give your partner a kiss on the forehead or cheek.
- Hold your partner close during moments of vulnerability.

## Practical Exercises to Enhance Love Expression

It's not fair to our partners to assume that they know that we love them. We have to show them because that's what love does. It is active. It is an exercise, something that you do. it is not passive. You see, love thrives on expression, and gestures, both big and small, are its language. When we embody love through our actions, we create an environment of emotional nourishment and affirmation. Each intentional act of kindness and thoughtfulness serves to reinforce the foundation of our relationships, forging bonds that weather life's challenges. Taking the time to articulate our love in meaningful ways means that we are dedicated to the growth and prosperity of our partnerships. This exercise allows us to explore the multifaceted ways in which we can tangibly manifest our affection, nurturing a dynamic and enduring connection. As we engage in this practice, we uncover opportunities to elevate our expressions of love, fostering an atmosphere of understanding, compassion, and joy. By actively engaging in this process, we cultivate a culture of gratitude, reciprocity, and mutual admiration, enriching not only our relationships but our own lives as well. The act of expressing love becomes a profound and illuminating journey—one that perpetually replenishes and rejuvenates the heart.

# Exercise 1: Letter of Appreciation

In this exercise, we explore the power of heartfelt appreciation through a delightful and thought-provoking scavenger hunt. The aim is to ignite the joy of acknowledgment and gratitude while embarking on a journey of love expression.

## *Step 1: Setting the Stage*

Gather a collection of readily available items such as sticky notes, colorful pens, stationery, and personal mementos. These will serve as your tools for crafting beautiful expressions of appreciation.

## *Step 2: Brainstorming Tokens of Gratitude*

Reflect on the characteristics, actions, and qualities of your partner that resonate deeply with you. Consider their virtues, strengths, and the multitude of ways they enhance your life. Subsequently, jot down these sentiments on the sticky notes—each note encapsulating a distinct reason for your heartfelt appreciation.

## *Step 3: Placement Strategy*

Once you have composed your assortment of declarations of gratitude, strategically place them in locations that will pleasantly surprise your partner. Consider areas they frequently visit, such as their dresser, the coffee maker, their workspace, or perhaps inside a bag or a book they are currently reading. The element of surprise will infuse a sense of delight and intrigue into the experience.

## Step 4: Essence of Surprise

After the placement of your tokens of gratitude, casually observe your partner as they uncover the hidden notes. As they discover each heartfelt message, bask in the glow of their reactions, expressions, and the warmth that emanates from the realization of being truly seen and appreciated.

## Step 5: Reflect and Amplify

Once the initial surprise has settled, engage in a heartfelt conversation about the scavenger hunt. Discuss the emotions and thoughts that surfaced during the journey and revel in the art of reciprocal admiration. This reflective discussion not only reinforces the nurturing power of gratitude but also deepens your emotional connection.

## Step 6: Reverberations of Joy

Take some time to bask in the resonance of this shared experience. Allow the joy of gratitude and love expression to linger, creating ripples of warmth and contentment that infuse your relationship.

# Exercise 2: Shared Journaling- Cultivating Intimacy Through Words

## Step 1: Selecting the Journal

Choose a journal or a notebook that resonates with both you and your partner. The journal itself can be a reflection of your combined tastes and styles, a harmonious melding of your personalities.

## Step 2: Setting the Tone

Select a quiet, comfortable space where both of you can openly communicate and share your thoughts without interruption. Create an ambiance that encourages relaxation and vulnerability, such as lighting a candle or playing gentle, soothing music in the background.

## Step 3: Commencing the Dialogue

Agree upon a schedule to engage in shared journaling—a time reserved exclusively for this joint activity. This could be a weekly or biweekly occurrence, allowing both partners the opportunity to reflect and express themselves without pressure.

## Step 4: The Art of Authentic Expression

During each session, take turns writing heartfelt messages, thoughts, reflections, and even creative expressions within the shared journal. Emphasize transparency and vulnerability, allowing your words to communicate your deepest feelings and desires.

## Step 5: Unveiling and Discussing

After each journaling session, take time to read and absorb one another's entries. Engage in a candid, authentic discussion about the contents—sharing your emotional responses, deepening understanding, and fostering a sense of emotional connection.

## Step 6: Nurturing Growth

As the shared journal becomes an integral part of your relationship, observe and celebrate the growth and evolution of your words and feelings. This moving practice allows for the cultivation of empathy, compassion, and a deepened bond through the power of shared expression.

This beautiful exercise offers a sanctuary for emotional vulnerability and intimate connection, affording both partners the opportunity to express themselves freely and unconditionally. When you and your partner do this together, you infuse your relationship with the potent elixir of open communication and enduring love.

## Love Language Challenge

The concept of love languages was popularized by Dr. Gary Chapman, who identified five primary ways that people express and receive love: words of affirmation, acts of service, receiving gifts, quality time, and physical touch. As we have discussed earlier, each of us has a primary love language that resonates with us the most, and understanding and speaking your partner's love language can greatly enhance your relationship.

In this exercise, you and your partner will take the Love Language Challenge to better understand each other's love languages and increase love expression in your relationship.

### *Step 1: Identify Your Love Language*

Take some time to individually reflect on your primary love language. Consider how you feel most loved and appreciated by your partner. Do you feel most loved when they offer words of affirmation, do acts of service for you, give you gifts, spend quality time with you, or engage in physical touch? Write down your primary love language.

## Step 2: Discuss Your Love Languages

Sit down with your partner and share your primary love language with each other. Discuss what makes you feel loved and appreciated, and listen attentively to your partner's love language. Take notes and ask clarifying questions to ensure you fully understand each other's love languages.

## Step 3: Love Language Action Plan

Together, create a love language action plan. Discuss specific ways you can express love to each other based on your primary love languages. For example, if your partner's love language is acts of service, you can offer to help with household chores or run errands for them. If your love language is quality time, you can plan regular date nights or uninterrupted time together.

## Step 4: Love Language Challenge

Set a love language challenge for yourselves. For the next month, make a conscious effort to express love to each other in ways that align with your partner's primary love language. Keep track of your efforts and the impact it has on your relationship.

## Step 5: Reflect and Reconnect

At the end of the challenge, take time to reflect on the experience. Discuss how expressing love in each other's primary love languages has impacted your relationship. Share the moments when you felt most loved and appreciated, and express gratitude for your partner's efforts.

WEEK 3: UNDERSTANDING YOUR LOVE LANGUAGE

## Claim Your Free Date Night Bonus Here!

*In the previous sections, we've touched on "date nights" a few times, and later in the book, we'll dive even deeper into why they're so essential. But I wanted to give you a head start! Since date nights are something I'm truly passionate about, I'm thrilled to share a special resource to help you bring more connection and joy into your relationship.*

*Simply scan the QR code below or head to https://booksforbetterlife .com/relationship-workbook to download **my Ultimate Date Night Planner**—absolutely free!*

*Inside, you'll find essential tips for keeping your relationship vibrant, along with a thoughtfully designed date night planner filled with beautiful ideas to inspire your time together.*

## Balance between Independence and Interdependence in a Relationship

Jasmine and Aaron have been together for a couple of years now, and things have been going relatively well until just recently. Spending time together is something that they have always loved doing, but Jasmine has started to feel a little like she is losing her sense of independence because she is spending more time engaging in Aaron's interests than her own. She is starting to feel a little like she's losing herself in this relationship, and it's starting to affect their dynamic together. Jasmine reached out to Aaron about these concerns she's been having, and they both came to the conclusion that they need to find that perfect balance between spending time together and maintaining their own identities.

What Aaron suggested was that they dedicate a day each week to pursue their individual interests and hobbies. Jasmine was ecstatic about the whole thing, so she booked herself a cooking class because that's something she's always wanted to try. Aaron signed himself up for a woodworking class because he'd never really had time for that. The arrangement was working out fairly well until Jasmine started to feel like she was barely spending any time with Aaron. She was quite busy, so it seemed that their schedules were never in sync What they then did was decide on a date night during the week. They agreed that they wouldn't talk about anything related to work. Instead, they would simply just focus on enjoying each other's company.

What they discovered after a while was that making time for their own interests as well as their relationship gave them a healthy sense of independence and togetherness at the same time. It made them both feel fulfilled as a couple and as individuals. They worked hard at this and continued to maintain balance as time went on, solidly committed to making the relationship work. Their story is a beautiful reminder of how balance and togetherness are key in a relationship. Regardless of how much we love our partners, we must still be able to maintain our own interests. When we are willing to communicate this effectively with one another, we will be able to find the balance that best works for all of us.

Independence in our relationships represents our own individual needs for autonomy, self-expression, and personal space. It is the desire to continue being ourselves while being one with our partners, and then interdependence or togetherness is the desire for closeness, intimacy, and shared experiences. It's about spending quality time together, making decisions together, and building a life as a unit. Independence has a very important role:

- Firstly, it allows us to continue growing in our own right, to continue to learn and evolve. It is what ensures that we don't lose sight of ourselves and our goals.

- Secondly, it enriches the relationship because when we maintain a strong sense of self, we allow our partners the opportunity to learn from and experience the world from our perspectives.

- It also reduces the need for codependency. Being overly dependent on a partner leads to codependency, which can be detrimental to the intimacy of a relationship.

- Lastly, independence leads to a healthy level of respect for each other's boundaries. Independence acknowledges that every person has their own needs and desires.

While independence is very important, we also have to maintain a sense of togetherness. Togetherness is the glue that binds intimacy through shared experiences, and that deep emotional connection allows us to grow closer to our partners.

Interdependence is also very important for making joint decisions. When we are in relationships, we have to make decisions with the other person in mind. It's not just about us anymore, but about them as well.

Independence means that there's someone there for emotional support, both in the good times as well as the bad times. It gives us a steady anchor to hold on to as we navigate our lives with many ups and downs.

Finding The Balance Between Independence and Interdependence

- It's important for each of you to have your own space and time for personal pursuits and self-reflection. Encourage each other to pursue hobbies or activities that bring joy and fulfillment independently. Whether it's reading a book, going for a walk, or pursuing a personal interest, carving out solo time allows each partner to recharge and maintain a sense of individual identity within the relationship.

- While it's crucial for partners to pursue individual aspirations, setting mutual goals can strengthen the bond between them. Whether it's planning a trip, saving for a shared investment, or taking up a new hobby together, working toward common objectives creates a sense of unity and shared purpose. This allows couples to experience growth and accomplishments as a team while still maintaining their individual identities.

- Be cheerleaders for boundaries. Encourage open discussions about personal boundaries and respect each other's need for space and autonomy. By setting and respecting boundaries, couples can foster an environment of trust and mutual respect, allowing both partners to thrive as individuals while nurturing their connection as a couple.

- Allowing each other to be as quirky and "you" as you are is key to striking a balance between independence and togetherness. Rather than seeking uniformity, celebrate the diversity that each partner brings to the relationship. Be open to learning from each other's perspectives and experiences, and use those differences to enrich your shared journey together.

- Remind each other to tend to your self-care needs. Whether it's hitting the gym, practicing mindfulness, or simply taking time for relaxation, nurturing individual wellness is crucial. By maintaining a healthy balance between self-care and caring for the relationship, partners can show up as their best selves within the partnership.

## Balancing Independence and Interdependence Through Shared Values: An Exercise

Aligning values is a crucial part of maintaining a harmonious and fulfilling relationship as well as the cornerstone for being able to maintain a good balance between independence and interdependence. Here's a step-by-step exercise for you to work on aligning your values:

**Step 1:** Encourage each other to individually reflect on your core values. This can include principles, beliefs, and priorities that guide your lives, such as honesty, family, career ambition, kindness, spirituality, or personal growth. Provide a list of common values as a starting point for reflection.

**Step 2:** Once each partner has compiled their list of values, come together and discuss which values are most important to each of you. Identify the values that you both hold in high regard. It's essential to approach this discussion openly and without judgment, allowing each partner to express the significance of their chosen values.

**Step 3:** Acknowledge that while many values may align, there might also be differences in values that are important to each partner. Use this as an opportunity to understand and appreciate your partner's perspective. Discuss any disparities and delve into the reasons behind why certain values hold significant meaning for each of you.

**Step 4:** After identifying both shared and differing values, work together to prioritize the most important values for your relationship. Discuss which values you both believe should be foundational in guiding your partnership. This can involve compromise and understanding as you navigate the impact of different values on your shared life.

**Step 5:** Craft a joint value statement that combines the prioritized values you both hold dear. This statement should encapsulate the essential principles that will guide your relationship and serve as a compass for decision-making and goal-setting. It should reflect the shared values that you've identified as key to your partnership's success.

**Step 6:** Move from discussion to action by aligning your shared values with specific goals and behaviors in your relationship. This can include making joint decisions, setting common goals, and establishing daily practices that reflect your shared values. Regularly revisit this value statement and ensure that your actions remain aligned with your mutual values.

**Step 7:** Schedule regular check-ins to review and reaffirm your joint value statement. This can be a part of your ongoing communication, ensuring that your relationship continues to be guided by the values that hold significance to both of you. Use these check-ins as an opportunity to celebrate your shared values and address any new insights or changes.

Love speaks through our actions. The things that we do and say to our partners to make them feel loved differ for each person. Love is attentive and unselfish in its giving. It's about the little moments, those seemingly small gestures that carry immeasurable weight in affirming our affection for the ones we love. Whether it's preparing a surprise breakfast, holding hands during a difficult moment, or simply listening without judgment, it all adds up to weaving a tapestry of shared emotions, understanding, and care.

In this chapter, we explored the ways in which love is expressed and, more importantly, how our partners receive it. It's often said that actions speak louder than words, and in love, this adage rings especially true. By examining how we communicate our affection through daily interactions, we can gain a better understanding of our partners' unique emotional language. This helps foster a deeper connection and a more harmonious relationship.

Understanding our own love language and that of our partner can illuminate the varying ways in which we express and receive love. Through this exploration, you can build a stronger bond by learning to speak and understand each other's love language more fluently. You enhance the depth and richness of your connection, creating a more fulfilling and enduring love. This understanding, woven into our daily lives, is what makes our relationships thrive. Remember, love is not just a noun; it's a verb—an action that is perpetually being defined and refined through the conscious choices we make each day.

## Notes

# Week 4: Building Trust

*"Love cannot live where there is no trust."*

— EDITH HAMILTON

You deserve to be in a relationship with someone who will take care of you. I am not just saying take care of you in a materialistic way, but someone who will take care of your soul, your well-being, and everything else that comes with you.

When I was still studying, I would occasionally dog sit for this sweet old lady, Barbara, and her husband, Cameron, or "Uncle Cam" as I called him. Their interactions together were the kind that made me believe in a soft and steady kind of love—a love that you can trust, a love that has your back, the kind of love that says, "Here, I took care of dinner tonight because I knew you'd be tired when you got home. I checked the tire pressure for you. I will be running late tonight, so I don't want you to worry."

Uncle Cam and Barbara had been married for over 50 years, and their love for each other was evident in the way they treated each other with kindness, respect, and consideration. It was the little things that stood out to me the most. Like the way Cam would always hold the door open for Barb or how she would always make sure he had his favorite snacks stocked in the pantry.

Their love was steady and reassuring, and it was clear that they had built a strong foundation of trust over the years. They knew each other's likes and dislikes, they knew each other's routines and habits, and they were always there for each other no matter what.

I remember one time when Cam had to undergo surgery, and his wife stayed by his side the entire time, making sure he was comfortable and taken care of. And when she fell ill a few months later, he was right there, making her soup and keeping her company until she felt better. Their love was unwavering, and it was clear that they had each other's best interests at heart.

In a world where trust is often hard to come by, witnessing their love was a reminder that it is possible to build a relationship based on trust and mutual care. It takes time, effort, and a willingness to put the other person's needs above your own at times. It also takes open communication, honesty, and the ability to forgive and move forward from past mistakes.

Building trust again in a relationship can be challenging, especially if it has been broken in the past. But it is possible with patience, understanding, and a commitment to making things right. It starts with small gestures, like being there for each other in times of need, showing empathy and compassion, and being reliable and consistent in your actions. It also involves being transparent and honest in your communication and being willing to work through any issues that may arise.

Trust is the foundation of a healthy and lasting relationship, and it is worth the effort to rebuild if it has been damaged. Just like Cam and his wife, it is possible to create a love that is steady, reassuring, and built on trust. And it is a love that is worth striving for.

## Identifying Potential Trust Issues

We are all human and messy and imperfect, and we come with a whole lot of baggage as well. So, it is completely normal that with our lived life experiences, we may find ourselves succumbing to those potential trust issues that work themselves into our relationships. Let's unpack some of the most common trust issues that we may be susceptible to:

- **Infidelity**: This is the most common trust issue in a relationship, and it happens when one partner engages in a physical or even emotional affair with someone outside the relationship.

- **Dishonesty:** This can take many forms, including lying, withholding information, or breaking promises. It can erode trust over time and lead to resentment and anger.

- **Financial Infidelity:** This is when one of you hides or mismanages money or financial resources without the knowledge or consent of the other partner.

- **Lack of Emotional Support:** When you fail to provide emotional support to the other, it can lead to feelings of isolation and mistrust.

- **Inconsistent Behavior**: This can be confusing and leads to mistrust in a relationship. This may include changing plans frequently or failing to follow through on promises.

- **Control Issues:** When one of you tends to control or manipulate the other partner, it can erode trust and lead to feelings of resentment and anger.

- **Privacy Breaches**: When one partner invades the privacy of the other, it can lead to feelings of mistrust and betrayal. This may include going through personal belongings, reading private messages, or stalking.

## Do You Have Trust issues?

Let's have a look at some of these to determine how far and wide your trust issues run. You may experience the following things:

- You exhibit overly cautious behaviors like a reluctance to take risks and put yourself in situations where you might be emotionally dependent on each other.

- You are overly critical of others and assume that everyone is untrustworthy.

- You're skeptical and suspicious, meaning you always jump to conclusions, question your partner's motives, always assume the worst of people, and snoop through your partner's belongings.

- You test your partner's loyalty by setting up situations to see how they will respond.

- You project your own insecurities by accusing your partner of being unfaithful and dishonest.

## *Identifying Your Areas of Mistrust*

One helpful exercise to identify areas of mistrust in a relationship is to reflect on your past experiences and take note of any recurring patterns or incidents that have caused feelings of mistrust or betrayal. You can also make a list of behaviors or actions that have caused mistrust in the past, such as lying or infidelity, and rate the level of trust that currently exists in the relationship regarding each behavior. It will also be helpful to have an open and honest conversation with your partner about any areas of mistrust and work together to identify ways to rebuild trust and strengthen the relationship.

## Addressing Jealousy and Insecurity

Yes, it is okay to expect your partner to bring warm and fuzzy feelings into your life, but what you cannot expect them to do is to make all aspects of your life feel warm and fuzzy. Only you can do that for you. If we make our partners solely responsible for that, it can easily lead to jealousy and insecurity.

Jealousy and insecurity are common issues that can arise in any relationship. While a certain amount of jealousy is normal and can even be healthy, excessive jealousy and insecurity can be destructive and can erode the trust and intimacy between partners. Jealousy can stem from a variety of sources, including past experiences, feelings of inadequacy, and fear of abandonment.

It can manifest in different ways, such as questioning your partner's loyalty, becoming possessive or controlling, or feeling threatened by your partner's relationships with others. Insecurity, on the other hand, can arise from a lack of self-confidence and a fear of rejection or abandonment. It can lead to feelings of inadequacy, anxiety, and low self-esteem and can cause you to doubt your worth and your partner's feelings for you. If left unaddressed, they lead to a breakdown in communication, frequent arguments, and even the end of the relationship. However, there are ways to manage and overcome these issues and build a stronger, more trusting relationship. Here are some tips to overcome jealousy:

- **Identify the root cause of your jealousy:** It is important to understand why you are feeling jealous in the first place. Is it due to a specific behavior or action of your partner, or is it based on past experiences or traumas? Identifying the root cause of your jealousy can help you to address it in a more constructive way. Use the journal prompts below in this chapter to get to the root cause of your jealousy.

- **Communicate openly with your partner:** Communication is key in any relationship, and it is especially important when it comes to addressing feelings of jealousy. Be honest and transparent with your partner about your feelings, and try to listen to their perspective as well.

- **Work on trust:** Building trust in the relationship can help to alleviate feelings of jealousy. This can be done by being honest and transparent with each other, following through on commitments, and being supportive of each other's goals and aspirations.

- **Avoid comparing yourself to others:** Comparing yourself to others can fuel feelings of jealousy. Instead, focus on your own strengths and accomplishments and celebrate the successes of your partner and others in a positive way.

## *Journal Prompts for Identifying the Root Causes of Your Jealousy*

It is advised to make these journal prompts individually to find your own answers. Afterward, it is good to discuss your answers with each other if you both struggle with jealousy.

1. When do you feel the most jealous? Try to identify specific situations or circumstances that trigger your jealousy. Was it something your partner said or did?

2. Consider your past experiences with jealousy in your relationships. Have you noticed any patterns or recurring themes?

3. What thoughts go through your mind when you feel jealous? Write down any negative or self-critical thoughts you have about yourself or others.

4. What do you think is the underlying cause of your jealousy? Is it related to feelings of insecurity, fear of abandonment, or both?

5. Think about the role of social media in your relationship and how it affects your feelings of jealousy.

6. How does your jealousy affect your behavior and actions? Do you find yourself acting out or engaging in negative behaviors?

7. Have you talked to your partner or friends about your jealousy? If so, what was their response, and did it help you feel better?

8. What are some healthy ways you can cope with feelings of jealousy? Think about things like self-care, mindfulness, or seeking support from friends or a therapist.

9. What are some things you can do to improve your self-esteem and self-worth? Consider activities or hobbies that make you feel good about yourself.

10. Think about how your partner can help you deal with your jealousy. Are there certain things they can do to reassure you or make you feel more secure in the relationship?

11. How can you communicate your feelings of jealousy to your partner in a healthy and constructive way? Consider using "I" statements and expressing your needs in a nonjudgmental way.

12. What are some positive affirmations or mantras you can repeat to yourself when you feel jealous? Write down a few phrases that help you feel more calm and centered.

## Trust Yourself First

Do you know if you trust yourself? Here are some signs that you don't trust yourself as much as you say you do:

- You have a very difficult time making decisions.
- You don't validate your own experiences.
- You value external opinions over your own.
- You shy away from speaking up for your beliefs and needs.
- You dwell on the mistakes that you have made.
- You try to control every situation.
- You criticize yourself.
- You silence your intuition.
- You have a very difficult time making decisions for yourself.

Self-trust is not trusting yourself to know all of the answers all the time, nor is it believing that you will always do the right things all the time. It's having the conviction that you will be kind and respectful toward yourself regardless of the outcome of your efforts.

It's normal to get it wrong at first because it's something that takes a while to get settled into, but with practice and a whole lot of patience, you can work on validating yourself and building that sense of trust in yourself again. This is how you do it:

- **Be gentle and kind with the parts of yourself that seek external validation.** Do not punish yourself. Be understanding and compassionate with yourself as you ease into the process of it all. For example, if you don't want to do something, but you find yourself thinking, *But people will love me if I do this*, gently tell yourself that you really don't have to please or try to please everyone. It's unrealistic to expect that of yourself.

- **Notice that there is a much wiser and more secure part of you that**

**can guide and lead the way.** See if you can get in touch with your much wiser self.

- **Practice listening to your wiser self by listening to your emotions.** Explore what it is that you are feeling and validate yourself in a way that makes the most sense to you. For example, say you're feeling anxious about an upcoming presentation. Take a moment to acknowledge and validate that feeling. Remind yourself that it's okay to feel nervous and that many people feel this way before giving a presentation. Then, try to identify what it is about the presentation that is making you feel anxious. Is it a fear of failure, a fear of being judged, or a fear of forgetting your lines? Once you've identified the source of your anxiety, you can work on addressing it in a constructive way.

- It's very difficult to trust your gut and to make decisions when you feel panicked and insecure. **Engage in regular practices that focus on nervous system regulation and learn how to calm yourself down at the first signs of overwhelm.** Say you're feeling overwhelmed by a big decision you have to make. You may notice that your heart rate has increased or your breathing has become more shallow. Instead of letting these physical symptoms continue to escalate, try practicing some nervous system regulation techniques. This could include taking deep, slow breaths, going for a walk in nature, or practicing mindfulness meditation.

- **When in doubt, ask for support from trusted others, but never value their opinions over your own.** Remember that you are the expert on your life. You are the one who ultimately knows what is best for you.

The more ownership that we take over our own feelings, responses, and behaviors, the more beautiful our lives become. Self-confidence, self-reliability, and self-trust all look a little bit like being willing to sit with whatever it is that you are experiencing, even when it is deeply uncomfortable. Stepping into the kind of relationship that you've always imagined requires owning all that you are and recognizing your worth. This can be a difficult process, as it may involve confronting uncomfortable emotions or facing your fears. However, with the guidance of love, you can push through this discomfort and develop a deep sense of self-trust. Here's an exercise I also want you to try:

Each day, set aside some time to reflect on your experiences and write down your thoughts and feelings. Begin by asking yourself a few questions, such as:

- What did I experience today that made me feel happy/sad/anxious/angry?
- What did I learn about myself today?
- What decisions did I make today, and how did they make me feel?
- What challenges did I face today, and how did I overcome them?

As you write, try to be as honest and transparent with yourself as possible. Don't worry about grammar, spelling, or punctuation—just focus on expressing yourself in a way that feels authentic and true.
Over time, you will begin to notice patterns in your thoughts and emotions, and you will become more attuned to your inner voice and intuition. You may also begin to recognize areas of your life where you need to build more self-trust, such as in your relationships, career, or personal goals.

Remember, this will take a while, but commitment is key. With practice, you can learn to trust yourself more fully and make decisions that are in alignment with your true self.

Self-trust is something that also requires a good measure of self-confidence. Here is another exercise you can do to build your self-confidence in increments.

1. Start by making a list of small goals you would like to achieve in the next week. These could be simple tasks like cleaning out your closet, organizing your desk, or trying a new recipe.

2. Choose one goal from your list and break it down into smaller, more manageable steps. For example, if your goal is to clean out your closet, your smaller steps could be to sort through your clothes, organize them by category, and donate any items you no longer need.

3. Set a specific deadline for completing each step, and hold yourself accountable by tracking your progress in a journal or planner.

4. As you complete each step, take a moment to acknowledge your achievement and celebrate your progress. This could be as simple as giving yourself a high-five or treating yourself to a small reward, like a favorite snack or a relaxing bath.

5. Repeat this process with each goal on your list, gradually increasing the difficulty of your tasks as you become more confident in your abilities.

Confidence is not something that will be handed to you on a silver platter, and you have to be intentional about working toward it. Work on it like your very life depends on it, and also remember that you don't have to be doing big things, just tiny little things. Those in themselves are big enough to make a difference.

## Managing Your Finances

Financial transparency is one of the most crucial cornerstones of building trust in a relationship. Money matters can be a common source of friction in any relationship, and a lack of financial transparency can contribute to feelings of mistrust, resentment, and even deception. When partners are open and honest about their finances, it builds a sense of security and stability in the relationship. This, in turn, allows couples to focus on other aspects of their relationship without worrying about the financial strain that can come from a lack of transparency. For most relationships, things go better when finances are going well, when bills can be paid, and when they can set some money aside for savings or investments. When both partners are transparent and accountable with their finances, they can work together to achieve their financial goals, make important decisions, and build a strong foundation of trust in the relationship.

## Money Talks Aren't Always Easy

Money talks are not always easy in a relationship because they can bring up a lot of emotional baggage and even trigger past traumas. For example, if one of you grew up in a family where money was a taboo topic and never discussed openly, you may feel uncomfortable talking about finances in your current relationship. Similarly, if you grew up in a family where there was a lot of financial stress, you may have a heightened sensitivity to money-related issues.

Also, a lot of us also have different values and priorities when it comes to money. For example, one partner may prioritize saving for a down payment on a house, while the other partner may prioritize paying off debt. These competing priorities can create tension and conflict if not addressed properly. Lastly, discussing finances can also reveal differences in income, spending habits, and debt. These differences often conjure up shame, guilt, or even resentment if not addressed in a healthy way. For instance, if one partner earns more money than the other, they may feel resentful if they are expected to contribute a larger share of the household expenses.

## *Having Conversations Around Money*

Those financial conversations aren't going to have themselves. You and your partner need to sit down and have those together.

- **Set aside time to talk:** Schedule a time when both partners can sit down and discuss finances without distractions. This can help create a safe and focused space for the conversation.

- **Practice active listening:** When discussing finances, it's important to listen actively to your partner's perspective and concerns. Avoid interrupting or dismissing their opinions, even if you don't agree with them.

- **Be honest and transparent:** Honesty is key when it comes to discussing finances in a relationship. Be transparent about your financial situation and any concerns you may have. This can help build trust and create a stronger foundation for your relationship.

- **Focus on shared goals:** Rather than focusing on individual priorities, try to identify shared financial goals that are important to both partners. This can help create a sense of unity and cooperation when it comes to managing finances.

- **Seek outside help if needed:** If financial conversations become too difficult to navigate on your own, consider seeking outside help from a financial planner or therapist. They can provide objective advice and support to help you and your partner work through any issues or concerns.

**Tips for Financial Planning**

- **Set shared financial goals:** Discuss and set financial goals together as a couple. This could include saving for a down payment on a house, paying off debt, or setting aside money for a vacation.

- **Create a budget:** Create a budget that outlines your monthly expenses and income. This can help you identify areas where you can cut back on spending and save more money.

- **Divide financial responsibilities:** Divide financial responsibilities between partners based on each other's strengths and interests. This could include one partner managing the bills and the other managing investments.

- **Plan for emergencies:** It's important to have an emergency fund that can cover unexpected expenses, such as car repairs or medical bills.

- **Review and adjust regularly:** Review your financial plan regularly and make adjustments as needed. This can help ensure that you're staying on track to meet your financial goals.

## Building Trust Through Little Things

Trust is built over all the little things—those things that are sometimes seemingly insignificant. Those are the things that matter because if you can be faithful in the little things, then you can surely also be faithful in the big things. Here's a list of little things that you can do to keep up that momentum of building trust between you and your partner.

- being punctual
- listening attentively
- being reliable
- showing appreciation
- being honest, even about small things
- keeping promises, no matter how small

## WEEK 4: BUILDING TRUST

- showing empathy
- being consistent in behavior
- being supportive during tough times
- sharing thoughts and feelings openly
- remembering important dates and events
- doing small acts of kindness
- being affectionate
- making time for each other
- being patient
- offering to help with tasks
- giving compliments
- respecting each other's opinions
- being forgiving
- being transparent about where you are and who you're with
- respecting personal space
- making decisions together
- being transparent about finances
- being accountable for mistakes
- taking responsibility for your actions
- making sacrifices for each other
- showing interest in each other's hobbies
- supporting each other's goals
- sharing the workload at home
- being a good listener
- apologizing when necessary
- respecting boundaries
- being trustworthy with secrets
- making compromises
- showing gratitude
- being open to feedback
- showing respect for each other's families
- standing up for each other
- making each other laugh

- being respectful in disagreements
- celebrating each other's successes
- being attentive to each other's needs
- being considerate
- being loyal
- giving the benefit of the doubt
- being dependable
- being thoughtful in gestures
- being supportive of each other's friendships
- showing love through actions
- being present in the moment

## Notes

# Week 5: Intimacy and Connection

*"Intimacy is a totally different dimension. It is allowing the other to come into you, to see you as you see yourself."*

— OSHO

I was reading a thread the other day where a writer asked people what intimacy means to them. There were a lot of different answers that stood out, but these are my favorites:

**Laughing laughter over a steaming coffee.** This reminds me of the love between my grandparents. I could almost feel the warmth of the coffee cup in my hands, the comforting aroma rising in spirals amidst our shared chuckles. It wasn't just the coffee—it was the ease in their conversation and the unspoken understanding between them. It was a moment unburdened by the weight of the world, a moment of pure connection. In this simple act, they were not just sharing a drink but also their thoughts, emotions, and vulnerabilities.

**Holding hands during a long walk by the ocean.** There's something remarkably intimate about intertwining your fingers with another person's as you traverse the sandy shore, with waves rhythmically crashing against the coast. The sound of the sea, the salted breeze rustling through our hair, and our silent, shared appreciation of the vast expanse before us—it creates a bond that transcends the physical touch, a connection that speaks volumes without words.

**Finding solace in the quiet moments, side by side, lost in a book.** In the subtle rustle of pages turning and the faint scent of aged paper, there is a tranquility that comes from being in the presence of someone you cherish. The shared silence is far from empty; it's a comforting embrace of mutual understanding and acceptance. It's a reminder that intimacy isn't always about grand gestures—it's often found in the unspoken, in the comfortable companionship of two souls at peace.

**Dancing together in the kitchen, intertwined in each other's arms.** The music fills the air, mingling with the aroma of our culinary creations. In the midst of our improvised steps, I'm struck by the gentle harmony of our movements, the unspoken language that flows between us. In the soft glow of the kitchen lights and the warmth emanating from our embrace, every sway and twirl speaks of a deep connection, a trust that allows us to truly let go and be vulnerable in each other's arms.

These snapshots of intimacy paint a very beautiful portrait of what it means to be truly connected—moments that transcend the physical and delve deep into the emotional, intertwining two hearts in a symphony of shared experiences and emotions.

# Physical Intimacy and its Role in Relationships

When we feel connected, we experience sexuality on a whole other level. When we feel safe, we allow ourselves to be less guarded. When we are open, we are able to talk about what we like, crave, and desire. When we unmask our vulnerabilities, we open ourselves to the willingness to try more things. When we feel like we are accepted, we adopt the belief that we are good enough sexually. When we feel desired, we want to touch, flirt, and build playful tension. When we trust, we are more open to receiving touch and pleasure. When we feel shown up for, we give back touch and pleasure. When we feel seen, we feel more confident, capable, and sexy too. When we feel respected, we trust that our bodies will be respected, too.

One of the most common barriers that couples face is not recognizing the direct correlation between physical intimacy and its role in relationships. The thing that most often shows up is that there is a lack of connection, a lack of safety, and an overall lack of intimacy in dynamics.

This often leads to couples feeling more like roommates, business partners, or acquaintances than lovers because of that deep hurt and resentment that has built up over time. One partner is struggling to feel connected to their partner because of that lack of physical intimacy, and this is where the disconnect happens. so then they end up in this vicious cycle where everyone is so focused on what they are not receiving that they don't realize that intimacy is actually all just about closeness and safety.

## Activities to Deepen Intimacy

Your relationship doesn't need to be crumbling apart for you and your partner to start working on your intimacy game. You can work on and build it even if you are in a good place. Here are a few of my favorite intimacy-building exercises that you can try together:

- **Soul gazing:** This one requires guts because it takes courage to really stare at someone in the eyes. To sit and really look at them. So here's what you do: You sit facing each other with your knees almost touching each other, and you hold eye contact for 3-5 minutes. You are allowed to blink, of course. Doing this small exercise will help you re-spark that fire and allow you to really see your partner. Like really see them.

- **Extend some cuddle time:** This is something so simple but so often ignored. Do you and your partner have a bedtime routine, or do you both just distract yourselves until you fall asleep? Whether before bed or just as you are about to wake up, having an extended cuddle session will do wonders for your relationship. You can play a favorite song in the bedroom or enjoy the silence—whatever works for you.

- **Uninterrupted listening:** Let your partner say whatever it is that they want to say; they can be talking about their day, what's been on their mind lately, or just about how they feel about you. Let them talk, and you simply listen. Sometimes, there is more shared understanding in intentional silence than when you are just responding to fill the silence.

- **A game of five things:** This is simple and quick and can be done absolutely anywhere. A common example of five things would be naming and mentioning five things that you are most grateful for or love about your partner. You can take turns alternating your five things or alternate each round. Its versatility makes it ideal because the only thing that will be limiting you is your imagination.

## *Make Time for Each Other*

A lot of us are blinded by the all-or-nothing mindset when it comes to making time for our partners. If we're being honest with one other, because of other life stuff that gets in the way, we may not always have the time to set aside more than 2 hours to spend with our partners. So when that happens, we must teach ourselves to be resourceful with the amount of time that we have. This is what you can do:

- Leave a little love note for your partner to find.
- Give a spontaneous hug or kiss.
- Send a sweet text message.
- Cook a meal together.
- Go for a walk or hike together.
- Watch a favorite show or movie together.

- Offer to do a small errand for your partner.
- Compliment something specific about your partner.
- Listen actively when your partner is talking.
- Share a favorite memory together.
- Plan a surprise date night at home.
- Offer to give your partner a massage.
- Do a small chore without being asked.
- Leave a thoughtful voice message.
- Send a small gift or token of appreciation.
- Create a shared bucket list of things to do together.
- Share a funny or heartwarming story from your day.
- Plan a picnic in the park or backyard.
- Take a spontaneous day trip together.
- Write down things you appreciate about your partner and share them.
- Have a technology-free hour and just talk.
- Offer to help with a task your partner finds challenging.
- Express gratitude for something your partner did.
- Create a playlist of songs that remind you of your partner.
- Share a laugh over a silly joke.
- Offer to take over a responsibility for the day.
- Whisper an "I love you" in your partner's ear.
- Share a small victory or accomplishment with your partner.
- Frame a favorite photo of the two of you.
- Watch the sunset or sunrise together.
- Explore a new hobby or activity together.
- Send a funny meme or GIF to brighten their day.
- Share a small treat or snack you know they love.
- Help your partner unwind after a long day.
- Pay attention to their preferences when making plans.
- Share a funny or heartwarming story from your day.
- Leave a surprise on their pillow.
- Create a scrapbook or photo album together.
- Offer a genuine compliment about something they did.

- Plan a fun and lighthearted activity together.
- Play a game or puzzle together.
- Plant a small garden or potted plant together.
- Write a love letter or email expressing your feelings.
- Cook breakfast in bed for your partner.
- Organize a surprise outing to a favorite spot.
- Share a special talent or skill with your partner.
- Take a moment to simply hold hands.
- Plan a date night at home with a special theme.
- Create a vision board for your future together.
- Simply say, "I appreciate you" and mean it.

## *Initiating Sex*

Initiating sex is an important part of any relationship, but it shouldn't fall only on one partner to put in all the effort, especially if sex equally means something to the both of you. But we also cannot ignore that initiating sex can feel incredibly tricky because there's so much potential misunderstanding and perhaps even rejection as well. If you and your partner communicate well enough, the likelihood of this happening is scarce. But if you're both looking for better ways to initiate that sexy time, here are some of my favorite tips:

- Plan… Plan… Plan…Let your person know that you are thinking about them. Sending them a naughty little text alerting them that you are thinking of them can prepare them for your advances.

- Make time for foreplay. Take this seriously. Invest in your person's arousal and your own, too, of course. Light the candles, put on some sexy music, give them a massage or some cuddles, or any other form of intimacy.

- Sometimes, introducing a new toy can be a fantastic way to get the ball rolling. Ask them if they want to see your new lingerie or shop around online for sex toys that you'll enjoy using together.

- Tell your partner what you want. They aren't a mind reader, and neither are you. Tell them how attractive you find them and what exactly it is that you want them to do. Novelty is a huge turn-on, so ask them if there is a new position that they want to try or even a new toy.

- Talk about sex often—what you want or what you don't want. Ask them how they like to be seduced. Some people like touch, while others prefer a more direct means of communication.

## *Pillow Talk and Desires*

Our partners don't come into the relationship knowing how to love us well; we teach them how to do it through communication. It works in the same way with our desires as well. We teach them what we want by being specific and opening up our voices. Here are a few prompts that you can use to open up that discussion:

- I've been thinking about trying (insert desire or experience here) with you. What do you think?

- Do you have any fantasies or desires that you've never shared with me?

- Can you describe your ideal romantic or intimate evening together?

- What is your favorite memory of our intimacy, and is there anything else you'd like to explore from that experience?

- If you could create the perfect romantic getaway for us, what would it look like?

## WEEK 5: INTIMACY AND CONNECTION

- Is there something specific you'd like more of in our intimate moments together?

- Is there a role-playing scenario or fantasy you've always wanted to try with me?

- What kind of physical touch or affection makes you feel the most loved and desired?

- Can you think of a time when you felt truly desired by me? How can we recreate or build upon that feeling?

- When it comes to our intimate connection, what are some things that you'd like to experience more of?

- What does "romance" mean to you, and how can we infuse more of it into our relationship?

- Are there any specific sensual or erotic activities you'd like to explore together?

- Do you have any thoughts on introducing new elements of playfulness or spontaneity into our intimate moments?

- How do you envision our physical and emotional connection evolving as we grow older together?

- What's something I used to do that you found incredibly arousing or romantic?

- What are your thoughts about incorporating more passion and excitement into our everyday lives and routines?

- Do you feel fully comfortable expressing your desires to me? If not, what can we do to improve that?

- Have you ever had a romantic or intimate experience that felt particularly memorable? What made it stand out?

- Are there any ways you'd like to deepen our emotional and physical bond in our relationship?

- If you could create the ultimate romantic evening for us, what would it entail?

Building and sustaining intimacy in a relationship requires the effort of more than one person in the relationship. It's something that cannot be done by one person alone. You and the other person both need each other. You need each other's time and effort. Remember that and make that the mantra and central theme in this connection that you are building together.

WEEK 5: INTIMACY AND CONNECTION

## Jumpstart Your Journey: Download the 30-Day Connection Challenge!

*By going to this link: https://booksforbetterlife.com/relationship-work book or scanning the QR code, you'll gain access to one of my all-time favorite challenges:* **the 30-Day Connection Challenge.**

*I created this with the hope that each day's small, thoughtful prompt would help you and your partner rediscover each other in new ways, creating a deeper, more meaningful connection. These daily challenges are designed to be simple but impactful—whether it's a moment of shared laughter, a heartfelt conversation, or a sweet surprise.*

*This challenge is more than just a series of tasks; it's an invitation to bring even more joy, warmth, and love into your relationship, one day at a time. I'm excited to share it with you as a free gift.*

*So go ahead, dive in, and let each day's prompt lead you to a stronger, more joyful bond together.*

## Notes

# Week 6: Overcoming Challenges

*"The strongest relationships are not always the ones that show no struggles, but the ones that grow through them."*

— UNKNOWN

Love doesn't mean an absence of conflict or confrontation. Love doesn't mean that communication will always be easy or that challenging conversations will never happen. Conflict, confrontation, and challenging conversations can be tools that are used to construct a solid foundation upon which our love can be built. In this chapter, we will explore the common challenges that we are most likely to face, and I'll provide you with practical tools and strategies to overcome them. When we embrace these challenges as opportunities for growth, we nurture a relationship that is resilient, supportive, and built to withstand the test of time.

## Common Relationship Challenges

Nowadays, it may seem like every relationship is falling apart at the seams. Couples often find themselves facing a myriad of challenges that can strain even the strongest of bonds. One common challenge is the lack of appreciation. Over time, you may start to take each other for granted, forgetting to express gratitude for the little things and failing to acknowledge each other's efforts. This leads to resentment and emotional distance, eroding the foundation of the relationship.

Financial difficulties are another significant challenge. Money matters can be a major source of stress and conflict, especially when there are differences in spending habits, financial goals, or unexpected financial burdens. Then there is boredom, that silent threat that gradually creeps in, causing us to feel disconnected and unfulfilled. Routine and monotony can dull the excitement and passion that were once central to the relationship, leading to a sense of stagnation and disengagement. Secret keeping can also be detrimental to a relationship. Whether it's withholding information, hiding emotions, or keeping significant aspects of one's life hidden, secrecy can erode trust and create a barrier to intimacy and genuine connection.

Additionally, a lack of responsibility within the relationship can lead to feelings of imbalance and resentment. When one partner consistently fails to fulfill their obligations or share the burdens of daily life, it can create a sense of unfairness and strain the partnership.

These challenges show in various ways within a relationship, often causing tension, emotional distance, and discord. They can lead to arguments, passive-aggressive behavior, withdrawal, and a general sense of dissatisfaction. However, it's important to recognize that these challenges are not insurmountable obstacles but rather opportunities for growth and positive change.

Understanding the root causes of these challenges is essential for addressing them effectively. Whether it's a breakdown in communication, unmet expectations, differing values, or external stressors, identifying the underlying issues is the first step toward finding solutions. let's Look at an exercise to see how we can be proactive with these.

## Proactive Problem-Solving

Proactive problem-solving is about taking a forward-thinking and collaborative approach to addressing challenges before they escalate. It's about identifying potential issues, understanding their root causes, and working together to find constructive solutions. This proactive approach empowers you and your partner to tackle problems head-on, fostering a sense of teamwork and mutual support.

You do this by scheduling periodic "check-ins" or "relationship meetings," You and your person can create a dedicated space to discuss any concerns, share feelings, and brainstorm solutions before small issues snowball into larger problems. This proactive communication strategy promotes transparency and prevents misunderstandings from festering.
As discussed during week 4, you can also budget and do financial planning together to address potential money-related challenges. Openly discussing financial goals, making shared financial decisions, and establishing a clear plan for managing expenses helps prevent conflicts related to money and help you work together toward your financial objectives.

Also, you both set realistic expectations and boundaries to prevent boredom and routine from creeping into the relationship. This might include planning regular date nights, engaging in new activities together, or consciously making an effort to keep the spark alive. By proactively investing in the relationship, couples can prevent feelings of disconnection and stagnation. Also, establishing a culture of open and honest communication around potentially sensitive topics, such as secrets or emotional needs, can be a proactive approach to preventing the erosion of trust.

Lastly, taking shared responsibility for the well-being of the relationship can be a proactive way to prevent feelings of imbalance and resentment. This might involve setting clear expectations for household responsibilities, childcare, or other shared commitments and regularly reassessing and adjusting these responsibilities to ensure a fair distribution of labor.

**Strengthen Your Bond: Download Your Free Weekly Check-In Sheet!**

*Just like you, my deepest hope is that, as you journey through this book, your relationship becomes even stronger and more connected. To support you along the way, I've created a **Weekly Check-In Sheet** that you can start using right now! This thoughtfully designed sheet has spaces for expressing gratitude, discussing challenges, celebrating wins, and setting intentions for the week ahead. It's a powerful yet simple way to nurture growth together, helping you put into practice all that you're discovering in this workbook.*

*To get started, just scan the QR code or visit https://booksforbetterlife.com/relationship-workbook to download your free sheet.*

*All that's left is to pick a day each week to fill it out together—an easy, meaningful habit that can make a real difference in your journey as a couple.*

WEEK 6: OVERCOMING CHALLENGES

## Resolving Disagreements

A thing that a lot of us still need to learn in relationships is how to meet each other in the middle. Now, what do I mean by this? Well, here are a couple of examples:

- Listen to each other's perspectives and try to understand each other's point of view.
- Recognize and acknowledge each other's needs and wants in a situation.
- Map your way through alternative solutions to a problem that both parties can agree on.
- Make an effort to find a solution that meets both your needs, even if it means giving up something.
- Maintains a level of respect about what you are willing to compromise on.
- Keep your hearts open or adjust your expectations to find common ground.
- Take turns making compromises to balance out the give and take in the relationship.
- Avoid ultimatums or threats to get your way in a situation.
- Be willing to apologize or forgive each other if compromises aren't successful or if mistakes are made.
- Focus on the larger picture of the relationship's health and longevity rather than just winning an argument.
- Be flexible and adaptable to changing circumstances or situations.
- Look at outside help as an option or mediation if needed to find a compromise that works well.

## *Finding the Middle or Your Ideal Place of Compromise*

Understanding the importance of finding "the middle" in your relationship is crucial. It helps you and your partner to communicate more efficiently, compromise, and maintain a healthy relationship.

1. To start with the exercise, grab a piece of paper and a pen. Write down what "the middle" means to you in the context of your relationship. Be as specific as possible. For example, it looks like not always doing what either one of us wants to do, but finding something that sounds ideal to both of us.

2. Once you have written down your definition, share it with your partner. Encourage them to do the same.

3. After each of you has shared your definition, discuss how you can work together to find "the middle" in your relationship. Brainstorm specific scenarios where finding "the middle" could be beneficial and discuss how you could approach those scenarios together.

4. Try working through scenarios together to find "the middle" in your relationship. For example, deciding where to go on vacation, how to divide household chores, how to spend money, etc.

5. After each scenario, share how you found "the middle" and how your personal definition of "the middle" helped you in the process.

6. Compromise is a lifetime of work. Encourage each other to take your personal definition of "the middle" and apply it to your relationship going forward, using scenarios from your own lives as opportunities to practice finding "the middle" together.

## Supporting Each Other in Challenges

Couples who are able to support and be by each other's side in those times when they each need it the most are the ones who have a stronger relationship. Emotional support is all about accepting your partner's emotions as valid and understandable. It's listening to them without ignoring or judging them for what they are feeling. It's what helps them feel heard and seen in the relationship. Emotional support will sound a lot like the following:

- I am here for you.
- How can I support you?
- I can see and understand why you are feeling that way.
- What do you need from me right now?
- Your feelings make complete sense.

## *Practical Ways to Offer Emotional Support*

You don't have to move mountains to let your partner know that you are there for them when they need you. It's the small stuff that really makes the biggest difference. Here are some small but big ways that you can be there for your partner when they are struggling:

- **Take them seriously.** Don't try to minimize their pain or their circumstance by making a joke out of it. If they are worrying about it or if it's affecting the normal state of their being, it must be a big deal to them. Even though you can't feel what they are feeling, you can let them know that, regardless, you are there for them.

- **Give them a hug, a kiss, or any form of physical affection that they might appreciate.** Remember to communicate this with them properly because different people respond differently to different levels of affection at different times.

- **Just offer them your love.** It is incredibly comforting and reassuring to know that your partner loves you even when things aren't all that great. Just make it clear that in all your presence, you are there to hold them both physically and emotionally. Sure, this might not fix everything, but it'll definitely make them feel less alone as they navigate this difficult time.

- **Check in.** Maybe they opened up about something, and you were able to offer a small bit of support at that time, but remember that some things take a while to get over. Ask them where they're at emotionally and if there's anything else that you can help them with.

## Forgiveness to Each Other

My gran tells me that the relationship between my granddad and her works because they wear forgiveness like a second layer of skin. It's not that they never make mistakes or have disagreements, but rather that they have learned the power of forgiveness in making their relationship thrive.

There have been moments when tensions ran high, harsh words were exchanged, and hearts were wounded. Yet, instead of holding onto grudges or letting resentment fester, they choose forgiveness. It's as if forgiveness is their secret weapon, a shield that protects their love from being tarnished.

I've witnessed countless instances where they've practiced forgiveness. Whether it's a small misunderstanding or a major disagreement, they always find a way to let go of the hurt and choose understanding instead. They understand that holding onto past mistakes only weighs them down and prevents growth.

Forgiveness, for them, is not a one-time act but a continuous practice. It's a conscious decision to let go of the past and focus on the present. They've learned that forgiveness is not a sign of weakness but rather a strength that allows their love to flourish.

Through forgiveness, they've created a safe space for vulnerability and growth. They've built a foundation of trust and understanding that allows them to weather any storm. It's not always easy, but they believe that the effort is worth it.

I will always remember the lesson they have taught me. Forgiveness is the key that unlocks the door to a healthy and thriving connection. It's a choice we can make to let go of the past and embrace a future filled with love and understanding. Forgiveness is freedom and not choosing it is choosing misery.

## Forging Your Way to Forgiveness

There's no formula, secret recipe, or real 10-step guide that will teach you to forgive. I think it's something that we have to actively participate in to understand. Nonetheless, here are a few tips that might help along the way:

- Start by acknowledging the pain and hurt you feel within the relationship. It's important to give yourself permission to feel these emotions and understand their impact on your connection.

- Be kind to yourself during the forgiveness process. Remember that forgiving doesn't mean forgetting or condoning the actions but rather freeing yourself and your partner from the burden of resentment.

- Try to understand your partner's perspective and motivations behind their actions. This doesn't mean you have to agree with everything, but gaining insight can foster empathy and facilitate forgiveness.

- Holding onto grudges only prolongs the suffering within the relationship. Make a conscious decision to let go of resentment and choose forgiveness as a way to release the negative energy and move forward together.

- If you feel comfortable, express your feelings to your partner. Honest and open communication can help in the healing process and pave the way for reconciliation and deeper understanding.

- Forgiving someone doesn't mean you have to ignore your own needs or tolerate harmful behavior. It's important to set healthy boundaries within the relationship to ensure that you both will continue to respect each other.

- Put yourself in your partner's shoes and try to understand their struggles and flaws. Cultivating empathy and compassion can soften your heart and make forgiveness easier, fostering a stronger bond.

## *Talking Our Way Through Forgiveness: An Exercise*

Forgiveness and healing are essential components of any thriving relationship. When we experience hurt or betrayal, it can create emotional wounds that impact our connection with our partner. Forgiveness mends those wounds and paves the way for healing and growth.

In this exercise, we engage in open conversation, focusing on forgiveness and healing within our relationship. These meaningful discussions and sharing of our experiences will deepen our understanding of each other's perspectives, cultivate empathy, and create a safe space for healing. Approach this exercise with an open heart, active listening, and a commitment to understanding and supporting each other. Be patient and compassionate as you navigate through the prompts, knowing that you might not get it right the first time around.

**Instructions:**

1. Sit down with your partner and take turns answering the following discussion prompts.

2. Listen attentively to each other's responses and be open to understanding different perspectives. Remember to approach the exercise with empathy, compassion, and a willingness to heal and forgive.

# WEEK 6: OVERCOMING CHALLENGES

**Discussion Prompts:**

1. Share a time when you felt hurt or betrayed in your relationship. How did it impact you emotionally and mentally?

2. Reflect on your journey toward forgiveness. What steps have you taken or are you currently taking to heal from the pain caused by that experience?

3. How do you define forgiveness within the context of our relationship? What does it mean to you?

4. Discuss the challenges you face in forgiving each other. Are there any specific barriers or obstacles that hinder the forgiveness process?

5. Share moments when you have felt forgiven by your partner or when you have forgiven them. How did it affect your relationship and personal well-being?

6. What role does empathy play in the forgiveness and healing process? How can we cultivate more empathy toward each other?

7. Talk about the importance of communication in the journey of forgiveness. How can we improve our communication to better understand each other's feelings and needs?

8. Discuss ways in which we can create a safe and supportive environment for healing and forgiveness within our relationship.

9. Share your hopes and aspirations for the future of our relationship. How do you envision forgiveness and healing playing a role in our growth together?

10. Finally, express gratitude for each other's willingness to engage in this exercise and for taking the opportunity to heal and strengthen your relationship.

## Working Through the Phases

As people, we will change and not change. We will struggle with the things that we struggle with and thrive at the things that we thrive at. While some of these are irritating, I find them oddly freeing because they reinforce the idea that we are not meant to be the same person throughout our lives. I know that this can be a hard truth to accept, especially if the changing person is our partner. The fear and uncertainty that arise from witnessing their transformation can be overwhelming. But perhaps, by embracing the truth that change is an inevitable part of life, we can find acceptance and discover a deeper understanding of ourselves and our relationship.

**Have a look at this example:**

Greer has always been the predictable one, a dedicated teacher who finds solace in her involvement with the church committee. However, recently, she has been feeling a stirring within her, a desire for change that she struggles to articulate. This newfound restlessness both excites and worries her as she wonders how her partner, Ethan, will respond to her evolving self. Will he still love and accept her for who she is becoming?

Ethan, known for his adventurous spirit, has always embraced change with open arms. Yet, as Greer decides to find a new way of living, he finds himself questioning their compatibility. Will their paths continue to align, or will their differences drive them apart?

One evening, as the sun sets and casts a warm glow across the room, Greer musters the courage to share her innermost thoughts with Ethan. With a gentle smile, she reaches out to hold his hand and says, *"Ethan, I've been feeling*

## WEEK 6: OVERCOMING CHALLENGES

*something stirring inside me lately. It's hard to explain, but I have this yearning for change, for something different in my life. I'm scared that it might affect our relationship, but I wanted to share this with you because you mean everything to me."*

Ethan listens attentively, his eyes filled with love and understanding. He squeezes Greer's hand gently and replies, *"Greer, I've noticed the spark in your eyes, the way you've been exploring new interests and passions. It's beautiful to witness your growth. Change can be intimidating, but please know that I'm here for you every step of the way. Our love is strong enough to embrace the evolving versions of ourselves. Let's embark on this journey together, supporting each other's dreams and celebrating the beautiful changes that life brings."*

In that moment, Greer feels a wave of relief washing over her. She realizes that she doesn't have to face her desire for change alone. With Ethan by her side, she feels empowered to embrace her evolving self and pursue her dreams. Ethan also realizes that. as scary as it is that she is changing, he is rather lucky that he is the one getting to witness this transformation firsthand. What a blessing it is.

In real life, that realization might not come together that easily, but in case you need some reminders, here are a few to give you a leg up:

- **Realize how lucky you are:** Yes, consider yourself blessed, as you have the front-row seats to witness the person you love transforming into the best version of themselves. You get to be their biggest cheerleader, supporting and encouraging them every step of the way.

- **Nurture their growth:** Take pride in being their guiding light, offering unwavering support and encouragement as they navigate the path of self-discovery.

- **Embrace the adventure:** Embrace the thrilling journey of change together, knowing that every twist and turn will only deepen your bond and create a more vibrant connection.

- **Cherish their uniqueness:** Celebrate the individuality that makes your partner shine, knowing that their evolution will bring new dimensions to your relationship.

- **Foster a sanctuary of acceptance:** Create a safe haven where your partner feels free to explore their changing self, knowing that your love and acceptance remain steadfast.

- **Empower their dreams:** Encourage them to chase their aspirations and pursue their passions, knowing that their success will be a testament to the strength of your partnership.

- **Embody love's resilience:** Embrace the truth that love can weather any storm, including the winds of change. Trust in the power of your love to adapt and grow alongside your evolving partner.

## Exercise: Navigating the Phases Together

Take some time to talk about your fears. Create a safe and open space for honest dialogue, actively listening to each other's thoughts and feelings. Use these prompts as a starting point for meaningful discussions on navigating the phases of change in your relationship.

### Conversation 1: Embracing Change

**Prompt**: Reflect on the changes you have individually experienced and discuss how they have impacted your relationship. Share your thoughts on embracing change and how you can support each other's personal growth.

**Tips**: Be open-minded, empathetic, and nonjudgmental during this conversation. Validate each other's experiences and express gratitude for the opportunity to grow together.

## Conversation 2: Compatibility and Shared Values

**Prompt**: Explore how your changing selves align with your shared values and goals. Discuss any concerns or fears about compatibility and brainstorm ways to nurture your connection amidst evolving circumstances.

**Tips**: Focus on finding common ground and shared aspirations. Emphasize the importance of open communication and compromise to ensure your values remain aligned.

## Conversation 3: Dreams and Aspirations

**Prompt**: Share your individual dreams and aspirations, considering how they may have evolved over time. Discuss how you can support each other's dreams while maintaining a sense of togetherness.

**Tips**: Encourage each other's passions and explore ways to integrate your dreams into a shared vision. Be supportive and offer constructive feedback to help each other achieve your goals.

## Conversation 4: Communication and Understanding

**Prompt**: Reflect on how your communication styles may have changed and discuss any challenges that arise from these shifts. Explore strategies to enhance understanding and maintain effective communication throughout the phases of change.

**Tips**: Practice active listening, empathy, and patience. Be willing to adapt your communication approach to accommodate each other's evolving needs.

## Conversation 5: Balancing Independence and Togetherness

**Prompt**: Discuss the balance between individual growth and maintaining a strong sense of togetherness. Share your thoughts on how you can foster independence while nurturing your bond as a couple.

**Tips**: Encourage each other's personal pursuits while finding ways to create shared experiences. Establish boundaries that respect both individuality and the need for quality time together.

## Conversation 6: Reaffirming Love and Commitment

**Prompt**: Reflect on your love and commitment to each other amidst the phases of change. Express your feelings, reaffirm your dedication, and discuss ways to keep your love alive and thriving.

**Tips**: Be vulnerable and express your love openly. Share specific ways you can show appreciation and support for each other, reaffirming your commitment to weathering any changes that come your way.

# Developing Resilience as a Couple

Love will always feel like love, even at its most challenging. This is what resilience teaches us; it teaches us that love is not just the easy, sunny days but also the storms and the dark nights. It's the unwavering commitment to weathering the trials and tribulations together, holding each other close when the world seems to conspire against us.

Resilience is the quiet strength that emerges when we find ourselves facing adversity. It is the courage to keep believing in the beauty of our love, even when circumstances threaten to dim its light. It's the determination to rebuild and grow stronger after every hardship, knowing that our bond is worth every ounce of effort. It's a thread of hope, reminding us that even in our most vulnerable moments, we are capable of rising above our challenges. It's the embrace that says, "I am here for you, no matter what," and the understanding that together, we can overcome the seemingly insurmountable.

It invites us to dance with the rhythm of life, knowing that each step, whether graceful or stumbling, is part of our shared journey. It's the melody that underscores our commitment, harmonizing the highs and lows into a symphony of unwavering devotion. It's the promise that we will stand tall together, our intertwined branches reaching for the sky, no matter what storms may come our way.

Resilience is the heartbeat of our love, steady and reassuring, guiding us through the uncertainties of life. It's the gentle reminder that we are not alone, that we are bound by a love that is as enduring as it is tender.

## *How Resilient Is Our Love? Quiz*

Answer the following questions honestly to assess the resilience of your love as a couple.

1. During challenging times, how often do we openly communicate our feelings and support each other?

- A) Always
- B) Often
- C) Sometimes
- D) Rarely

2. When faced with conflicts, how likely are we to find solutions and compromise rather than hold onto grudges?

- A) Always
- B) Often

- C) Sometimes
- D) Rarely

3. How do we usually handle major life changes or unexpected events (e.g., job loss, relocation, illness)?

- A) We face them together and adapt as a team.
- B) We struggle but eventually find our way.
- C) We tend to blame each other and experience a lot of stress.
- D) We often feel overwhelmed and distant from each other.

4. When one of us makes a mistake, how do we approach forgiveness and moving forward?

- A) We openly communicate, forgive, and work on rebuilding trust.
- B) We need some time, but eventually, we reconcile.
- C) It takes a while for us to move past it, and trust may be affected.
- D) We struggle to forgive and often hold onto resentment.

5. How do we support each other's individual goals and aspirations?

- A) We actively encourage and support each other's dreams.
- B) We try to be supportive, but it's challenging at times.
- C) We have different goals and struggle to understand each other.
- D) We feel unsupported in pursuing our individual aspirations.

6. In the face of external pressures or criticism, how do we stand by each other?

- A) We defend and support each other unconditionally.
- B) We try to support each other but may feel overwhelmed.
- C) We tend to blame each other under pressure.
- D) We often feel isolated and unsupported.

7. How do we prioritize quality time together, especially during difficult periods?

- A) We make a conscious effort to nurture our bond and spend meaningful time together.
- B) We try to find time, but it's often challenging.
- C) We struggle to connect and find quality time together.
- D) We often feel distant and disconnected.

8. Reflecting on our journey together, how do we view the strength of our love during tough times?

- A) Our love grows stronger through adversity.
- B) We've had our ups and downs but have managed to endure.
- C) We've faced significant challenges and have struggled to maintain our connection.
- D) Our love feels strained and fragile when facing hardships.

**Key:** For each question, assign the following points:

- A) 3 points
- B) 2 points
- C) 1 point
- D) 0 points

**Interpreting your score:**

- **18–24 points**: Your love is highly resilient, showing strength and adaptability in the face of challenges. Keep nurturing and cherishing it.

- **12–17 points**: Your love has resilience but may benefit from intentional efforts to strengthen your bond during tough times. Think about these areas where you might support each other more effectively.

- **7–11 points**: Your love may currently struggle to bounce back from challenges, but this is an opportunity to work together and build greater resilience. Consider seeking support and guidance to strengthen your relationship.

**Tips for making your love more resilient:**

- Share your life news—the good, the bad, the ordinary, and the in-between. Sharing is what makes us feel less alone; it makes us feel connected.

- Let go of grudges and prioritize forgiveness to build a stronger foundation for your love.

- Show genuine interest in each other's aspirations and be a source of encouragement and motivation during both successes and setbacks.

- Prioritize quality time together, especially during challenging periods. Dedicate moments to connect deeply, share experiences, and strengthen your emotional bond.

- You are a team. Remind each other that it is you and your partner against the problems, not the problems against the two of you.

- Remind each other of your commitment to weathering life's storms together, reinforcing the understanding that your love is worth every effort and sacrifice.

I guess there's a lot that I can say to end this chapter, but I want to keep it short. For what it's worth, I hope that you keep your heart turned toward the good things, the true things, and the loving things. That is, after all, what love is about.

# WEEK 6: OVERCOMING CHALLENGES

## Notes

# Week 7: Creating a Lasting Love Story

*"Love is not about how long you've been together, but how you show love every day."*

— UNKNOWN

*You have love, and I hope that you keep falling in love with it.*

*I hope you keep falling in love with the way that it looks at you.*

*Or the way that it so tenderly holds you on your bad days.*

*I hope you keep falling in love with the way it makes you feel alive,*

*With the way it teaches you to thrive,*

*With the way it helps you grow and strive.*

*I hope you keep falling in love with the way it brings you peace,*

*With the way it makes all the worries cease,*

*With the way it helps your soul release.*

WEEK 7: CREATING A LASTING LOVE STORY

*I hope you keep falling in love with the way it inspires you,*

*With the way it helps you see the world anew,*

*With the way it makes all your dreams come true.*

*Love is the force that keeps us going,*

*It's the light that keeps us glowing,*

*It's the magic that keeps us flowing.*

*Remember that love is enough.*

*So keep falling and falling in love with it,*

*And let it lift you up like a dove,*

*For in love, you'll find everything you've been dreaming of.*

This is just a reminder from me to you because love stays, and love grows when we nurture it. When we are loud and boisterous about how we show it, each in our own way of course. Keep working on your love and you'll see and notice how it changes and how it grows.

# Setting Goals for the Future

The momentary bliss in our relationships is absolutely wonderful. Those are the moments where the pressures of tomorrow are simply just irrelevant. However, it's important to have those talks about the future. I think the last thing that any of us want is to find ourselves in a position where we are with this person and realize that what we both want for the future is completely different. Setting goals in our relationships is how we show commitment to one another; it's how we demonstrate that we care about the relationship and that we aren't just dragging our partner along until the next best thing comes along.

We can set both short- and long-term goals. Our short-term goals are the milestones that we set for ourselves and want to achieve in a relatively short period of time. These can be things like dancing, staying more connected by talking more on the phone or having more regular date nights. It's things like that, or perhaps taking more advantage of your love languages so that you better connect with each other. It's deciding that you're going to spice up your sex life and schedule time to have fun and enjoy each other's company!

The long-term goals, on the other hand, are the ones that focus on the bigger picture. The goals and aspirations that you set for yourselves in the long term ensure that you continue building a fulfilling and lasting partnership. Some examples of long-term relationship goals can include building a strong foundation of trust and mutual respect, maintaining a healthy and fulfilling emotional connection, supporting each other's dreams and aspirations, and working together to create a shared future. It can also involve goals related to marriage, starting a family, or growing old together.

## Discussing Your Vision for the Future Together: An Exercise

Despite what Disney might portray, the likelihood that you and your partner want different things is probably quite big. So, if you don't sit and work and plan through these together, both of you might find yourself at a point where you start to think, *Oh dear, I've lost myself in this relationship.* So, how do we go about setting goals to ensure that neither of us ends up settling for something that we don't really want?

**Brainstorm**: Both of you will write down things that you want to achieve either career-wise, concerning children, regarding home ownership, or things that you expect from each other. You are allowed to set a time limit for some of these things, and it doesn't matter if you don't get to everything.

Pick two or three things from the list. These should be the ones that both of you really care about, the ones that you want to turn into a reality.

**Compare**: Let's just say that your three home goals are to own a house, have a large garden, and have a home studio. Your partner's list is to live in Greece for a while, buy a house with a wine cellar, and live in a village. This would give you the idea that both of you have different ideas about where you want to live and how you want to live, but it is possible that you can get the things that are important to you. Maybe your partner will return the favor one day.

**Create the goal**: Now you have to turn the outcomes of the previous step into a goal that you can both get behind, e.g., get into a house in Greece with a garden. Then you start researching how much you need to save, career situations, and maybe some other valuable lessons or things to consider when living in Greece.

**Here are a few final tips:**

1. Motivate each other. You're going to need it on the days when it all feels pointless.

2. Make sure your goals are SMART.

- **Specific**: Your goals should be clear and specific, answering the questions of who, what, where, when, and why. Vague goals are harder to achieve because they lack clarity.
- **Measurable**: Your goals should be quantifiable so that progress can be tracked and measured. This involves establishing concrete criteria for measuring progress toward the attainment of each goal.
- **Achievable**: Your goals should be realistic and attainable. While it's good to set ambitious goals, they should still be within reach given the

resources, time, and constraints available.
- **Relevant**: Your goals should be relevant and aligned with broader objectives or aspirations. They should matter to your individual setting and contribute to overall success.
- **Time-bound**: Your goals should have a specific time frame or deadline for completion. Setting deadlines helps create a sense of urgency and provides a clear target to work towards.

3. Talk through things and emotions that you're feeling with each other. You don't have to do it all alone, you are in a relationship to help one another!

4. Make room for your personal goals, too.

WEEK 7: CREATING A LASTING LOVE STORY

## Plan Your Future Today: Download the Free Love Goal Planner!

*To make setting meaningful goals in your relationship even simpler, I've crafted a special resource just for you: the Future Love Goal Planner Worksheet. This in-depth guide is designed to help you and your partner map out a shared vision for your relationship, complete with practical tips and a flexible, customizable format where you can fill in your unique goals together. Imagine the excitement of creating a roadmap for the future you both envision!*

*For instant access to this free resource, simply scan the QR code or head to https://booksforbetterlife.com/relationship-workbook.*

*Start planning the future you both deserve—one intentional step at a time.*

## Integrating Hobbies and Interests

As much as you and your partner are separate individuals, you are also a united team. Embracing each other's hobbies and interests can be an enriching and fulfilling way to strengthen your bond and celebrate your unique identities. Here are some creative ways to integrate your individual hobbies and interests into your relationship:

- **Take the time to get to know each other's worlds, and encourage them to do the same with yours.** Whether it's joining them for a cooking class, attending a sports game together, or learning a new craft, sharing these experiences can deepen your understanding of each other and create new, meaningful memories.

- **Find ways to merge your passions and talents to create something unique together.** If one of you loves photography and the other enjoys hiking, plan outings to capture breathtaking nature shots. If one of you is a music enthusiast and the other loves writing, consider composing songs or poems together. Collaborative projects can be incredibly rewarding and strengthen your connection as a couple.

- **Show genuine interest in your partner's hobbies and accomplishments.** Whether it's attending their art exhibition, cheering them on at a marathon, or simply listening attentively as they share their latest project, your support and encouragement can make a significant difference. Likewise, openly express your enthusiasm for your own hobbies and endeavors and invite your partner to be a part of your journey.

- **Be open to expanding your horizons and acquiring new skills.** Encourage each other to step out of your comfort zone and try something new. Embracing a learning mindset can lead to mutual growth and a deeper appreciation for the diverse elements that make up your relationship.

## *Strengthening Your Connection Through Shared Interests*

Shared interests have a remarkable ability to strengthen the bond between you and your person, fostering a sense of unity and creating a shared narrative that deepens emotional connection. When you engage in activities that you both enjoy, you build a reservoir of shared experiences, inside jokes, and cherished memories that serve as the foundation of your relationship. Whether it's a mutual love for hiking, a passion for cooking, or a shared interest in travel, these common pursuits provide opportunities for meaningful interactions, communication, and collaboration.

Here are 20 new things you can explore together to further enrich your shared experiences and strengthen your connection:

- Take a dance class together.
- Volunteer for a cause you both care about.
- Plan a weekend road trip to a nearby destination.
- Try a new outdoor adventure such as kayaking or rock climbing.
- Attend a live music or theater performance.
- Learn a new language as a couple.
- Sign up for a cooking or mixology class.
- Embark on a DIY home improvement project.
- Start a small garden or plant a tree together.
- Join a book club and read and discuss books together.
- Take a fitness or yoga class as a duo.
- Attend a wine- or beer-tasting event.
- Explore a new cuisine by cooking a meal from a different culture.
- Plan a game night with friends or family.
- Visit a local museum or art exhibit.
- Try a new water sport, such as paddleboarding or snorkeling.
- Take a photography workshop and capture moments together.

- Create a vision board or set mutual goals for the future.
- Attend a workshop or seminar on a topic of mutual interest.
- Plan a surprise date night for each other, taking turns to design unique experiences.

## Support Each Other's Ambitions

Your partner was their own person with their own dreams before you. You are not responsible for breaking them down or keeping them away from those dreams. Instead, you must be the wind beneath their wings, propelling them toward their aspirations while standing alongside them as a source of unwavering support and encouragement. Just as a gentle breeze empowers a soaring bird, your belief in your partner's ambitions can lift them to new heights, allowing them to pursue their goals with confidence and determination. Embracing your roles as each other's champions, you can nurture an environment where both of you feel empowered to pursue your individual aspirations while fostering a deep sense of mutual respect and admiration.

Supporting each other's ambitions is akin to tending to a garden filled with unique, flourishing plants. Each of you represents a distinct flower with its own set of needs and aspirations. By nurturing and nourishing each other's dreams, you create an environment that allows your collective garden to thrive, fostering a sense of fulfillment and growth within your relationship. Just as a gardener tends to the diverse flora with care, attention, and patience, you must cultivate an atmosphere of encouragement, empathy, and understanding to ensure that both of your ambitions can flourish.

By openly discussing your individual goals, aspirations, and the steps needed to achieve them, you can gain a deeper understanding of each other's ambitions. Furthermore, like a network of interconnected roots, your support system intertwines, providing stability, strength, and nourishment to each other's dreams. As you provide unwavering support and celebrate each other's milestones, you foster an environment where both of you can thrive, propelling your relationship toward new heights of mutual fulfillment and success.

## Being More Encouraging to Your Partner

- Celebrate your partner's progress, no matter how small.
- Offer words of encouragement when your partner is feeling discouraged.
- Show interest in your partner's goals and ask about their progress.
- Help your partner brainstorm ideas and solutions to challenges they may be facing.
- Offer to be a sounding board for your partner to bounce ideas off of.
- Provide resources or contacts that may be helpful in achieving their goals.
- Offer to help your partner with tasks related to their goals.
- Give your partner space and time to work on their goals without interruption.
- Show appreciation for the effort your partner is putting into achieving their goals.
- Help your partner stay organized and on track with their goals.
- Provide positive feedback and constructive criticism when asked.
- Offer to be a cheerleader for your partner when they need extra motivation.
- Celebrate milestones and successes along the way.
- Help your partner stay accountable by checking in on their progress.
- Offer words of affirmation and support when your partner faces setbacks or failures.
- Help your partner create a plan of action to achieve their goals.
- Provide emotional support when your partner feels overwhelmed or stressed.
- Help your partner prioritize their goals and break them down into manageable tasks.
- Offer to be a partner in achieving your shared goals.
- Show your partner that you believe in them and their ability to achieve

their goals.

## Personal Growth

In your relationship, there has to be enough room left for you. You can't give all of you to your partner. You need to be able to know how to meet yourself so that you know how to meet their needs sufficiently as well. You don't have to self-abandon. Here are some tips on how to do just that:

- **Set boundaries and stick to them:** It's important to establish and maintain boundaries in your relationship to ensure that your needs are being met and that you are not sacrificing your own well-being for the sake of the relationship.

- **Prioritize your own happiness:** While it's important to consider your partner's feelings and needs, don't forget to prioritize your own happiness and fulfillment. Make choices that align with your own values and desires.

- **Honor your own feelings and emotions:** It's okay to feel what you feel, and it's important to acknowledge and validate your own emotions. Don't ignore or suppress your feelings in order to avoid conflict or keep the peace in the relationship.

- **Stay connected with your support system:** Maintain relationships with friends, family, and other loved ones outside of your romantic partnership. These connections can provide additional sources of support and fulfillment in your life.

- **Pursue personal growth and development:** Set goals for yourself and actively work toward achieving them. Whether it's furthering your education, pursuing a new hobby, or working toward a promotion at work, personal growth can help you maintain a sense of independence and fulfillment.

- **Take responsibility for your own happiness:** While your partner can contribute to your happiness, ultimately, it is up to you to create a fulfilling and joyful life for yourself. Take ownership of your own well-being and actively seek out experiences and opportunities that bring you joy.

- **Embrace your individuality:** Celebrate the unique qualities and traits that make you who you are. Don't feel pressured to conform to your partner's expectations or mold yourself into someone you're not in order to please them.

- **Trust your instincts:** Listen to your inner voice and trust your own judgment. If something doesn't feel right in the relationship, don't ignore your instincts. It's important to honor your intuition and advocate for your own needs and boundaries.

## Commitment and Closing

Love loves to be affirmed. Love stays, and it grows stronger when we tell it that we want it just as much as they want it. I guess what I am trying to say is that you mustn't ever make your partner second guess where they stand with you. Tell them how you feel about them. Reaffirm your love for them because you get to love this beautiful human being. You get to do life with them, and they get to experience life with you as well. Maybe you know that you should reaffirm your love for them, but you don't know what to say or how to choose your words. I have you covered here:

- I appreciate the way you always support me, even when things get tough.
- You make me want to be a better person every day.
- I feel so lucky to have you in my life; you bring so much joy into my world.

- You are my rock, and I'm grateful for your unwavering strength.
- I cherish the special moments we share together, and they're the highlights of my life.
- Your kindness and compassion inspire me to be more empathetic and caring.
- I'm constantly amazed by your intelligence and the way you see the world.
- You are truly unique, and I love every little thing about you.
- I feel most myself when I'm with you. You allow me to be completely authentic.
- You have a way of making even the ordinary days feel extraordinary.
- I love the way you make me laugh, even when I'm feeling down.
- You are my partner in every sense of the word, and I wouldn't have it any other way.
- Your love gives me the strength to face any challenge that comes my way.
- I'm grateful for your patience and understanding, especially when I'm not at my best.
- You are my best friend, confidant, and soulmate all rolled into one, and I love you more than words can express.

## Lasting Love Story Manifesto

*Dear future us,*

*It's probably 10 or so years from now, and we imagine that we are just as in love as we are today, if not more. As we sit down to write this letter to you, our future selves, we are filled with anticipation and excitement, curious to know how our lives have unfolded and how our love has grown over the years. We hope that we have weathered life's storms together, emerging stronger and more connected than ever.*

As you write your own letter to your future selves, consider including the following elements:

- **Reflect on your journey:** Take a moment to reflect on the journey you've been on together so far. Recall the challenges you've overcome, the milestones you've celebrated, and the memories that have shaped your relationship.

- **Express gratitude:** Express gratitude for the love and support you've received from each other. Acknowledge the ways in which your partner has enriched your life and express appreciation for the moments that have brought you closer together.

- **Share your hopes and dreams:** Share your hopes and dreams for the future, both individually and as a couple. Describe the life you envision for yourselves and the goals you aspire to achieve together.

- **Affirm your commitment:** Reaffirm your commitment to each other and the strength of your bond. Remind yourselves of the promises you made to each other and the values that serve as the foundation of your relationship.

- **Express your love:** Above all, express your enduring love for each other. Use this opportunity to speak from the heart and reaffirm the depth of your affection and devotion.

May this exercise serve as a timeless reminder of the love that binds you together and the dreams that continue to inspire you. Here's to the next chapter of your love story, filled with new adventures, wholesome memories, and a love that grows stronger with each passing day.

## Notes

# Bonus: Your Free Gifts

You've likely come across the bonuses several times throughout the book. If you want more tools and tips, these are your go-to guides. I'm offering these bonuses exclusively to my readers as a special thank you for your purchase. Below, I've listed them once more, giving you one last opportunity to download them for free:

- **The Ultimate Date Night Planner** – My planner, filled with ideas and tips to make every date night feel like your first date again (*$9.99*).
- **My Nurturing Self-Care Guide** – Your guide with meditations, yoga poses, and self-care lists to recharge yourself and strengthen your relationship (*$12.99*).
- **The Future Love Goal Planner Worksheet** – A worksheet with tips and a simple format to set and track your personal relationship goals together (*$15.99*).
- **Weekly Relationship Check-In Guide** – Your weekly check-in template to discuss successes, challenges, and goals for the week ahead (*$12.99*).
- **The 30-Day Connection Challenge** – A 30-day challenge with daily prompts to help you reconnect in simple, meaningful ways (*$19.99*).

**Total Cost /** *$71.95* **- FREE!**

To receive these exclusive **bonuses,** go to: https://booksforbetterlife.com/relationship-workbook

Or scan the QR code:

# Conclusion

Love is lovely. There's nothing quite like loving someone and being loved in return. As we come to the end of this workbook, it's important to reflect on the journey we've taken together. Throughout these pages, we've delved into the depths of what it means to truly connect with another human being and to foster love, understanding, and empathy in our most cherished relationships.

Love is a journey, an evolution of emotions and experiences that grow and mature over time. It's a dance between two individuals, a symphony of laughter, tears, support, and compassion. Through this workbook, we've explored the intricacies of communication, the art of compromise, the beauty of forgiveness, and the resilience of the human heart.

As we conclude, it's invaluable to recognize that love is not without its challenges. It's in these moments of adversity that we find the true strength of our relationships. We've learned that love is not always easy, but it is always worth it. It's in the hard times that we discover the depths of our commitment, the extent of our courage, and the boundless capacity of our hearts to heal and love again.

This workbook has been a guide, a companion on your journey to nurturing and understanding love. It has provided tools and exercises to help you navigate the complexities of relationships, foster deeper connections, and build a strong foundation for enduring love. As we close this chapter, remember that love is a continuous learning experience. It requires ongoing effort, dedication, and patience. It's not about finding perfection but rather finding someone with whom you can grow, evolve, and create a meaningful life.

In the end, love is about the little things—the quiet moments of understanding, the shared laughter, the supportive embrace, and the unwavering commitment to one another. It's about building a life together filled with love, respect, and kindness. As you take the wisdom gained from this workbook into your life, may you continue to cultivate love in its purest and most beautiful form. Always remember that love is lovely, and it's a gift to be cherished, nurtured, and celebrated.

*If you are open to discovering more about yourself, scan this QR code now to find my other books:*

# References

Fishman, S. (2022, July 22). *3 Power dynamics in relationships and how to overcome them*. Psych Central. https://psychcentral.com/relationships/power-dynamics-in-relationships

Harvey, S. M., Beckman, L. J., Browner, C. H., & Sherman, C. A. (2002). Relationship Power, Decision Making, and Sexual Relations: An Exploratory Study with Couples of Mexican Origin. *The Journal of Sex Research, 39*(4), 284–291. https://www.jstor.org/stable/3813229

Mbweza, E., Norr, K. F., & McElmurry, B. (2008). Couple decision making and use of cultural scripts in Malawi. *Journal of Nursing Scholarship, 40*(1), 12–19. https://doi.org/10.1111/j.1547-5069.2007.00200.x

www.ingramcontent.com/pod-product-compliance
Lightning Source LLC
LaVergne TN
LVHW020437070526
838199LV00063B/4773